M000201491

BeingTribal

practicing life in one-degree shifts

Rena Whittaker

BeingTribal
Published 2019 by Your Book Angel
Copyright © Rena Whittaker

All rights reserved. No part of this book may be reproduced, stored, or transmitted by any means—whether auditory, graphic, mechanical, or electronic—without written permission of both publisher and author, except in the case of brief excerpts used in critical articles and reviews. Unauthorized reproduction of any part of this work is illegal and is punishable by law.

The characters are all mine, any similarities with other fictional or real persons/places are coincidental.

Printed in the United States
Edited by Keidi Keating
Layout by Rochelle Mensidor

ISBN: 978-1-7330436-8-7

DEDICATION

To my loving family, especially my amazingly
wise children and precious grandchildren
who are my truest loves.

To all of my tribal women, especially Kim, Simone,
Vicki, Siri, Cristina, Serene, Louise, Rachel, Tammy,
Karen and Rachael... who continually lift me up and
empower me to find the magic!

Introduction

It's dark in here, except for the thin strip of light sneaking in through the folding closet doors. I am little. Still wearing clothes marked by Ts. I'm hiding. He wants to play the game. Closing my eyes so tightly that only white shadows show in the darkness. I pray a wish to myself: *Be small, be small.* It seems too challenging to breathe. *Be quiet.* There is a pounding so loud in my ears. It's my heart pounding, my whole-body thumping with each beat. I am trying to listen for him but the pounding is too loud inside my head. Too loud. My throat hurts like it's been tied in a knot. The air is thick and each breath takes time to inhale. Time I don't think I have. I can see little specks of dust in the thin line of light and I wish it was magical dust, to shrink me small. I am trying not to breathe loud. If he can't find me, I don't have to play the game. I don't want to be bad again. My little body is pressed up against the wall in the closet, legs pulled up against me, knees under my chin, arms tightly wrapped around my legs. Pounding heart. The pounding is too loud. He will hear it. *Disappear into the wall.* I press hard

5

against the wall, so it can steal me away from this place. Just be small, shrink down to the size of shoes and hide inside them.

I can hear that shaky iron railing on the stairs moving. I cover my mouth, so I can't make a sound. I hear a noise like a sob inside my head; my hands now tightly wrapped over my mouth. I can feel tears on my cheeks, but I don't remember crying them. *Disappear into the wall.* He is walking up the stairs, into the hallway. He is whispering my name and I press harder against the wall. *Be small. Be quiet.* I can hear him in the room and he is standing outside the closet, his shadow partially blocking out the stream of light that holds no magic. He whispers my name like he is singing a song. He is laughing, and his voice sounds thick like peanut butter. The light from the door goes dark and his hand is on the door and he peeks in. *Be small.* He slowly opens the doors. Light floods in and I watch it betray me—uncovering me slowly, beginning at my toes, and it's too bright. I look up at him. He is smiling, and I am found. His hand reaches for me like an invitation to dance. I start to cry but I make no noise, no calling for help. I am not small enough to hide and there is no magic and his hand grabs mine and pulls me up... I gasp and wake up.

It is 1983. I am a junior in high school and lie in bed trying to shake the feeling of thickness. Verifying with my eyes that it was just *the* dream and it was a long time ago, I try to wade through the haze of tastes and smells from my past, to feel any sense of safety I can find.

Each time I would have the dream, it would leave me entirely exhausted. My hands would be numb from being clenched so tightly in my sleep. Nausea often followed, and with it, the feeling of being exposed, like secret diary pages I wish I could burn away, made public. I remember lying in bed one morning, looking up as the light streaming into my room and seeing the dust floating in the air, knowing that magic doesn't exist. It was not possible to disappear or hide; it was only possible to be numb.

I grew up learning to exist in the world. It was easier to not feel my skin. Be numb to get through the days but not too numb, still paying attention in order to respond when called upon. Shape my lips into a smile and try to look happy. Tuck away my rotted-out self like neatly folded socks in a drawer. Like a robot, remember each day to look happy, be funny, and no one will really notice me.

Everyone knew that little girls were supposed to be pretty and quiet and always look happy. These weren't words spoken to me, but I learned by watching. Pretty, nice, clean girls get attention and praise. They are loved and protected. Pretty, nice, clean girls are adored and dressed up. I tried to look happy and act funny, too. I couldn't be pretty, but I could be funny. I had two older sisters and they were pretty and funny, and they loved me. My parents loved me, too. But only because they didn't know my secret.

When I look at my life in terms of BeingTribal, I know that my family was my first tribe. This is where I learned how to read signals from others and respond to them. My need to understand "acting and not feeling" came after the abuse. In fact, I became very good at sensing someone's next move. I learned how I was supposed to respond to happiness, pain, love, and fear. The fight or flight signals I sensed helped, even as a child, to develop a strong emotional barometer. Like a mathematical equation if x=y then smile and, if required, laugh. This constant equation helped me define how I would respond to the world around me. Not authentically, but at least to hide away my shame and guilt.

Growing up in my family, there was a lot of love and a lot of secrets. We didn't share our secrets about the drinking or the yelling, about the panic or the fear. We just put smiles on our faces. You make your family proud by keeping the secrets. Smile, fold your napkin in your lap when people are watching, and everything will be fine.

Our grandparents, especially my dad's parents, were mine and my sisters' saving grace. They believed in us. They kept us safe. Our parents built a house next door to their house, on the same block, so we were always close to them.

Grandma Pearl was our fierce protector. She loved us completely. She was a devout Catholic and she taught us to be strong in our faith. She was also Chinook Indian, and her spiritual strength was felt, not just seen. Most importantly, she taught us about standing up for those without a voice. She was devout in her belief that every single person deserved respect and dignity. She believed that we were all equal in God's eyes. Our Grandpa John was kind and fun-loving. He taught us to garden and to fish. He didn't go to church yet had his own spiritual strength. He resonated kindness and honesty. He believed that actions speak louder than words and you are what you do. He didn't have a lot of time for big talkers. Grandpa was an electrician by trade and he could fix anything. He used to sing vaudeville songs that my grandmother didn't approve of and he would make us laugh. He chewed tobacco and kept a can by his chair in the living room. He was a tall, thin man and grandma was short and round. Their house was where love lived.

My mother said that when I was a toddler, I used to crawl out of my crib in the middle of the night and walk next door to my grandparents' house, standing outside in their yard crying. Grandma would come and pick me up, put me in bed with her and call my mother. My mother told me that eventually my mom and dad turned my crib upside down to keep me in bed at night.

My parents divorced when I was three. They both loved and hated each other. I remember a lot of sadness around me.

We spent much of our time with Grandma Pearl and Grandpa John. They bought us school clothes and took us on camping trips and we were loved. Our life was happy with them.

After the divorce, we lived with our mother and we moved several times during the next few years. Dad stayed in the house next to his parents and my mother struggled to raise the three of us girls. We moved from apartment complex to apartment complex. We stopped going to Catholic church because mom was asked to leave after the divorce.

My mother tried to balance it all while working. She had a few good girlfriends. Being divorced in the late 1960s must have been very isolating. My mom started to create a new life for herself. This is when he found me. He was the son of one of my mother's friends. I remember him being kind and funny. He was nice to me and he always paid attention to me even when my sisters didn't want to play. He made me giggle, until he didn't anymore. I don't remember every time, but I do remember the first time.

9

We were in a room somewhere. People were in the same house, but we were alone. He was taking my hand and putting it on his pants and I didn't want to touch it or put it in my mouth, but it happened anyway. I will never forget him telling me after it was over that *now* I was a very bad girl and I shouldn't have done "it" and he was going to tell my mom and she wouldn't want me or love me anymore.

I wonder now if that is what someone told him when he was a child like me? *Your mommy or daddy won't want you anymore.* In that simple moment, the secret was kept secure. Those simple words—*no one will love you if they know you are bad*—created one of the tapes that kept playing in my head and would help hold me hostage for decades. He wanted to play the game every chance we were together, and no one seemed to notice. I was invisible and now I was bad, and I learned to be numb. *Close your eyes so tight that only white shadows show in the darkness. Go away deep in my mind. Little girls are clean and pretty and good. And you are none of those things.*

He brought me to meet a friend one day. I was a something of a gift to his friend, to be bad with him. I remember his friend looked at me with disgust and said no. My little mind created a tape again: *He doesn't want you. No one wants you.* I was not so lucky in other offerings.

Looking back now, every adult that should have been watching was on autopilot. I kept this secret for years. I never told my parents what happened during that time. Not until I was in my early twenties. It took me nearly two decades to convince myself that it was okay to tell. It was easier to just pretend back then.

When I was still very young, I saw a commercial on television one Saturday morning. It was for a pretty little doll that sat upon a pedestal and had a glass dome over her to keep her clean. She was so pretty and neat and perfect. I wanted to be her. I wanted to be pretty and protected. I wanted to be clean and kept safe from dust and dirty hands.

One summer before I started first grade, we moved to an apartment complex in Milwaukie, Oregon. There was a pool and lots of single parents with children. I had new friends and they were all like me. From divorced parents, poor, broken, and we saw each other. There were a lot of boys in the complex, too. Older boys. I kept my distance. I remember being chubby then and people would make comments like, "She'll grow out of her baby fat." People looked at me differently now, at least that was what I believed. I was sure that they could all see the grime under my smile. The rotted out little girl who had to hide and pretend to be someone else. I developed a habit of silently "re-mouthing" words after speaking them. I would say a sentence and then I would repeat it without sound. One of my sisters asked me why I was doing that. I didn't realize I was, and I remember practicing really hard to not repeat myself. I became hyper-vigilant about what I was doing. I didn't want anyone to think I was broken somehow. I needed to be more like that little doll under the glass and not let them see me, the rotted out little girl.

I began creating the *me* I wanted everyone to see. I learned to lie about how I felt and pretend I was "normal."

It was my birthday and I was in second grade. My dad was coming to take me to dinner. Mom had me all dressed up and I sat by the door on the chair waiting. Soon my dad would be there, and he would see me and pick me up and hug me and hold my hand and take me to dinner. He had a fancy plane and maybe he would fly me in the plane. I sat on that chair, excited for the night to come. I sat on that chair and waited for him. I waited even after my mother told me to not wait any longer.

Does he know about me? Does my dad know that I am rotted out inside? I remember my mother trying not to cry when she told me that my dad probably wasn't going to come to take me to dinner and I knew he must have known my secret. I knew my mom didn't know because she got me all dressed up and she wouldn't do that if she knew. I crawled into bed and tried to feel numb. *Just go to sleep and stop the pain. Hide, inside, screaming, raging, just stop this loud uneven circus ride, spinning too fast...stop the nausea and just sleep safe for a while.*

There was one girl who was my best friend. Her name was Lisa and she was also trying to hide. Lisa and I did everything together. Third grade was a year in turmoil. I got in trouble for missing over 60 days of school. My mother would leave for work and I wouldn't go to school. One day, Lisa and I went to an apartment where some older boys were. They were upstairs in a bedroom and watching one of their parent's porno films on a reel to reel projector. I felt like I couldn't breathe, and I was immediately sick to my stomach. My ears were ringing, and I felt like I had walked into a dangerous pool of snakes. I ran out of the apartment and Lisa followed. I went home to my room and sat on my bed, wrapping my arms around my knees and crying. *How did they know about me? How did they know that I was bad?*

12

The boys later made jokes about me running away. There was one boy who was always leading around this group of boys. When he would see me by the pool, he would make comments to me like, "When you get older, watch out." He reeked of cologne and he didn't know my mom, so I would hide from him. I knew he saw the ugly part of me. He saw the rotted-out part. I ran back to my apartment crying and my mother asked me what was wrong. I couldn't tell her. I lied. I learned to laugh when I wanted to cry. It was my first exceptional skill. I learned to lie before I ever learned to tell the truth.

During the summers, we spent time at Grandma Pearl's and Grandpa John's house. You could play in the dirt and make mud pies and be loved. We always ate lots of food and made friends with the neighborhood kids. You didn't have to be anything but yourself there. Manners were important, but happiness was paramount.

My mother's parents were kind and loving, too. They lived on a golf course in a large beautiful home and they had lots of parties. Down in the basement, they had a wet bar and a pool table. Their house was always immaculate, and their friends were nice. You had to be clean there. Grandpa Fred was joyful and very involved in his community. Everyone knew him. Grandma Laura was beautiful and stylish. She was like me in some way, too. I didn't realize until later that she was delicate in a far-off way. She had pain in her eyes of a forgotten dream and she was a doll under the glass cover, too. I think we saw each other. My grandmother's glass dome was very well decorated. She only showed what she wanted people to see. Grandpa Fred was a local business leader and politician. I thought

13

he was famous. When we visited their house on the golf course, we would get dressed up and go to the country club for dinner. Grandma Laura would always compliment me if I looked slender and pretty. No comment meant no approval, at least in my eyes.

I became an experienced decorator of my glass cover. I became the entertainer, the funny girl. Be pretty or funny, be thin and entertain, the glass cover was constantly being redesigned. Creating what I wanted everyone to see, covering the rot and displaying the new me. The girl who didn't belong, who was rotted out inside, that girl I kept hidden from everyone—she was not to be seen.

The early fall of my fourth-grade year we moved to a small town to my mom's first new home that she bought. I remember her saying that she was going to start over and I thought I would start over, too. I would be new, too. I could pretend that I was clean and pretty and happy.

I was starting fourth grade in a new school and I was new to everyone. No one knew me here. I had new friends and I felt safe. That didn't last long, as my teacher had me tested because I didn't pay attention in school. I was too busy being funny. She informed my mother that I was slow and possibly retarded and then she told some kids in the class that it was important they be nice to me because I was slow. I had to take a special IQ test and my mother talked to the new teacher and a counselor about me. My mother had a new best friend, too. She was a fifth-grade teacher at the same school I attended. She sat me down in front of my mother and told me that I wasn't retarded, I was just lazy. I was the problem. I was sent to speech therapy because I couldn't pronounce my Rs. Now, I was ugly and stupid

14

and lazy and dirty, all at the new school that I was going to start my "new" me in. My mom told me she loved me, and it was going to be okay but I knew it wasn't. I knew I was ruining our new start.

There are moments in your life when you realize that God or Love is speaking to you through someone. Not only because you see it in their eyes, but also because you can feel it. My first recollection of a moment like that was when I went to see my dad, which meant I spent the weekend at my grandparents' house. I was out in the garden, with Grandpa John, weeding around the flowers that outlined the vegetable garden and he asked me how my new school was. I sat down in the garden and lowered my head in my hands. I was ashamed to tell him, but I couldn't lie to my grandpa. I told him that my teacher said I was retarded and another one said I was lazy. He said, without pause, "Nope, then they both are retarded and lazy. Everyone can see that you are as smart as a whip and a hard worker." Then he stopped, knelt in front of me, and raised my chin up with his hand, so I was looking into his eyes. He said, "Listen to me. Don't ever let anyone tell you who you are or who you aren't. What you can do or what you can't do. You are going to do great things. You have just got to prove them all wrong." I knew he probably had to say those things to me. And we went back to weeding. But I didn't dismiss it altogether. Maybe he was right? I just had to prove it. I figured that since he knew me my whole life, and he didn't think I was stupid or lazy, maybe I could be good. I could prove them wrong. It was a fleeting moment, but it was a start to many moments in my life where I felt the possibility of who I could be. The moments when you see or feel the possibility of great things. Those perfect moments when your heart is full and you feel empowered. It was one of those moments.

My new school was a kindergarten through eighth grade school. I spent the rest of my time in school trying to be funny but not exceptional. I learned that when you try to be above average, people pay attention to you and that was not what I wanted. I just wanted to be liked and to be someone else. I just wanted to look like other people and if I did, then I was keeping my secret safe. I was going to be exceptionally average. I was very good at that.

High school was another new beginning and there was a new pressure to be pretty and thin. I wasn't either. A friend I had met over the summer took me to her church youth group that had a choir and it was my first experience at really praying. I read the Bible. It was my first introduction outside of my grandmother to faith and finding a higher power to pray to. I was surrounded by goodness and I felt safe.

High school was similar to my grade school years. I was an average student who was known for being nice, silly, and undedicated. I had a new tribe in high school and I met my best friend, Diana. She was wise beyond her years and kind. She taught me about hope and that anything was possible, and if I didn't trust and believe in myself first, no one else would. Diana knew all about challenges in life as she was paralyzed from a car accident the year prior. Diana also always told me the truth. She and her family became my second family. Diana was also my first authentic friend. She called me on my bullshit and we loved each other like sisters, and we still do to this day.

I hadn't learned yet about being authentic, though. I had become such an expert at keeping my glass cover coated with false images, and if I was caught in a lie about how normal I was, it would be quickly replaced with a new lie. I had become exceptional at lying.

I barely had good enough grades to get into college and I couldn't wait to get away, but I was not prepared to be at college. During that same time, I met my first serious boyfriend, Michael, and I was in love. He was fun and exciting, and I never knew that being intimate could be so wonderfully passionate. There were moments when I began to see the possibility of who I could be. There was a strength in enjoying my body as a woman. It was no longer something that betrayed me. I began to feel more comfortable in my own skin.

I met two girls in my dorm and we confided in each other about our lives at night. They became my college tribe. One had bulimia and threw up everything she ate and the other slept with every guy like she was fighting a war. They were my people because they, too, felt rotted out inside. I began to experiment with drinking but when you are drunk you say too much, so I was careful to keep my illusion intact.

Then my life changed. At least, it began to change in a one-degree shift. I went home for a long weekend and my mom gave me a cassette tape set that she had bought at a business conference. It was a career track seminar tape set entitled *Self-Esteem and Peak Performance* by Jack Canfield. I listened to those tapes over and over and over again. It was my first introduction to creating visual signs of what I wanted my life to become. I learned that we all make mistakes and to not let my past define my future. I could recite almost every word he spoke. It was like my new faith. I could change my life. The wisdom found on those tapes slowly set up residence in my world. I would listen to the tapes and then write down what I wanted to do. I began to practice creating visual cues in my life. I loved the stories he told about being authentic and that I had the power to create the kind of woman I wanted to be. I know those tapes were my first step in being honest with myself that I needed help. That I could tell someone who wasn't a friend. It still took me another two years before I went to see a counselor. Those tapes set the stage for me to finally seek help.

I decided to move home after winter term. I worked the summer and next fall I enrolled in a private college in the city, close to home. I reconnected with my friend, Diana from high school and I felt whole again. I met wonderful people at my new college and they were all very focused on their futures. I continued listening to those tapes and I began creating vision boards of what I wanted to become. I would pull out images from magazines and write in my journal, and I became dedicated in school. No one cared what my childhood was like, they were only interested in the present moment of each day and what they wanted their future to look like.

You know the old saying, "One step forward, two steps back?" That was true for the next several years of my life. I finished school and moved to Southern California and I went from one disastrous relationship to another. I lost my focus on doing great things and began to party and date. I had a unique ability to date men who were selfish and cruel. When I met a nice guy, I was dismissive and mean until he became cruel to me. After four years, I had enough and I moved to Oregon near home.

I sought out counseling for the first time and was given a workbook about adults surviving sex abuse, and finally I told my parents. I told my mom first. She didn't seem to believe me but she told me she loved me and I should let it go. That night I went to my father's house; he had been clean and sober for nearly 16 years by then and he suggested I attend an Alcoholics Anonymous (AA) meeting with him sometime… and then he left the room. I went back to my apartment and cried and laughed then went out to a bar with friends and tucked the day away in my sock drawer under the haze of beer, tequila, and cigarettes. I began having panic attacks and more nightmares – more than usual, and I sent myself to counseling, again. The counselor really listened to me and had me journal about my story. To free write as often as I could, how I felt, what scared me, what I wanted my life to look like. Each week I wrote a letter to my child self, telling her how much I loved her and how it wasn't her fault. I asked him if I should go to a group session for sexually abused women and he told me he didn't believe that would be the best thing for me, and instead he sent me to a female therapist who taught me new skills on reprogramming my brain, ditching those images, smells, and tastes that haunted me. Those sessions slowly changed my life. I had to practice my new skills. I wrote letters to my childhood self about what I was doing to protect her and how, when I had children, I would never let them be hurt.

I met my first husband on New Year's Day several months later. When we started dating seriously, I told him about my past. I even asked him to read some of my journal pages, so he knew what a mess he wanted to marry. I know I was trying to push him away, but he didn't leave so we got married. Within four years we had two beautiful children. I began to make changes and make even more mistakes, but I discovered something beautiful in life—that magic does exist, and it comes from love... loving my children and loving myself. After six years our marriage fell apart and neither of us had the skills to put it back together, so I ran from it. It took me a second divorce within the next ten years of struggling to realize that in order to change my life, I needed to practice new habits. I learned that perfection is not possible and replacing old fear-based beliefs with new habits will change your life, but it will take time. Change is a process that starts with a decision that is revisited again and again. Lasting change takes time and commitment. It takes patience and grace for yourself and all those you bring into your life.

I began to see the being I was created to be, and all the fear, guilt, and shame were heavy weights I no longer wanted or needed to carry. I had to learn how to peel the layers of old tapes away, like peeling an onion. I had to decide what kind of woman I wanted to become. The magic in this world exists all around us and we have to make a choice to welcome it into our lives.

I learned the importance of having a tribe around you. You can't be your own counselor – you need more than your own perspective to guide your life forward in a healthy way.

In the book you are about to read, I will be sharing with you the ways I have changed my life. I will share with you what has helped me. How you cultivate a tribe – having the *right* people around you in your journey, and how you can work with your tribe to share wisdom with each other and then pay that wisdom forward. I will also be introducing you to the wisdom that helped shape my life with video interviews on our website, beingtribal.com, as well as links to additional information and resources.

Life is beautiful and full of love, endless possibilities, and so much magic that it can't be contained. You can do this and live a life of greatness, filled with peace, compassion, abundance, and grace.

Chapter One

"A little step may be the beginning of a great journey"

— Unknown

There are four beliefs I know to be true. 1. Love is powerfully real, and it conquers hate every day and twice on Sunday! 2. Change can only start when you begin to love yourself first, before anyone else. 3. We need each other. 4. Everything is possible.

BeingTribal, practicing life in one-degree shifts, is about transforming your life with the help of your tribe. Transforming is a massive word. It means to make a thorough or dramatic change. You may only want to fine-tune or adjust your life, and that's okay. I had to truly change mine, from top to bottom. I knew that if I didn't transform my life, I was only going to be existing in life and I don't think I could have survived that. It starts with you. The process of deciding what you want your life to look like and feel like Then you can cultivate your tribe. You must learn to put yourself first. Then the tribe. This is not being selfish, rather SELF-FULL.

23

BeingTribal is a practice of how tribes work in our lives. This book is about how to fall in love with yourself and cultivate a tribe that empowers you to continue that journey of transformation in love.

Together, you and every member of your tribe will learn to pay attention to life and be present in the world. You will learn to manifest the life you want. By paying attention, you begin to live in the practice of life, practicing your life in one-degree shifts. This is not a 'lose 20 pounds in a week' kind of a book. This is about making sustainable changes over time that are empowered by the shared wisdom of your tribal members.

As humans, our soulful purpose is to love and lift each other up. It is also to grow and learn from each other, to soar higher than our past generations, soar higher with purpose.

Together, your tribe's collective wisdom, love, and good intent will be transformational. It is inevitable!

How we create our tribe is also about the strategy of putting you first. Focusing on you then your family, your tribe which will inform and connect with your community and ultimately your world.

24

In a professional setting, your tribe is your team and you add in your organization before your community, as seen below.

BeingTribal is a practice...

Chapter Two

BACK TO THE BEGINNING

"If three of us travel together, I shall find two teachers"

— Confucius

"We learned early in our existence that ice is cold and fire is hot..." That is how I usually begin talking about the simple wisdoms shared in tribes. We have lived in tribes for the last 200,000 years. The focus has always been evolving, surviving and thriving, loving and protecting each other.

We shared our wisdoms through storytelling, all to propel our tribes forward. That human connectivity, the feeling of belonging, has always been a powerful force. It has moved our tribes forward in continued existence and development.

It is just as powerful of a need today. We need to feel connected, to be part of something greater than ourselves. We are stronger individually when we feel connected.

26

Whether the tribes are personal or professional, when we feel part of something important and we see how it affects our lives for the better, everyone succeeds!

When we connect with others, there is a powerful human energy exchange. This energy exchange can alter how our minds process thought, and our bodies function. In an article by Mr. Dr. Suzuki entitled "The Body Electric," Mr. Suzuki writes about the human conduit and how humans emit enough electrical current to affect another living organism and everything around us affects us as well. *Many people, regardless of their belief in energy transfer, can attest to a person or group of people "draining" their energy. The fact of the matter is that humans can absorb and emit electrical current, which can have more of an effect than you may imagine. In some cases, it could change the path of one's day and possibly even one's life.*

As we begin to cultivate our tribe and even look at our existing relationships; how someone affects our energy, this is something to pay attention to. How our surroundings affect our energy is just as important. As you slowly transform your life, check in with yourself about how your energy feels physically, emotionally, and mentally as it relates to the people around you and your environment. Your body informs you in life and part of BeingTribal and practicing life in one degree shifts is about tuning into your body and listening to it. Does your environment or the people around you give you energy or drain you? Do you feel mentally foggy? Does your body feel sluggish? Just as it is critical to fuel your body with the right foods and water, it is equally as important to pay attention when there is an energy shift because of where you are and who you are with. The more you practice this "tuning in" the easier it will become to detect what gives you energy and what takes it away. As technology has advanced, especially in the last two decades, we have become more disconnected and even addicted to short-term interactions on social media. That has become our drug of choice. We find ourselves living in a world that is unlike any we have ever seen before. Of course, there have always been times of conflict, where hate and bigotry have ruled our societies. Now, however, our connection is more impersonal and allows for the divisiveness and competitive rhetoric, working to tear each other down rather than lift each other up. This happens on a daily basis and is applauded by our created society.

For years I have been searching for authentic connections;I long to trust and have faith in others. Larger group connections, where even if we disagree, we can still find common ground and trust each other. As humans, we want to know that when we do the right thing and live with good intent, we are surrounded by people who support and love us, even if we don't agree.

It has become far too easy to sit behind a screen and launch into demeaning and cruel words anonymously from self-created identities. I want to shout from the rooftops, *let us not allow the worst part of our humanity to have the loudest voice. We can persevere to create voices of love, wisdom, and compassion to love each other and lift each other up because that is what we were created to do!* It is what we were born to do—tribes of peoples working together in one world. Small tribes, joining together to create even larger tribes where we celebrate our differences, where we come together to listen and walk in each other's shoes rather than ignorantly judge what we do not know.

It's time to change the belief that being thin, rich, and famous is immensely more important than being loving, wise, and kind.

BeingTribal is a call to action, a movement, returning to our sole purpose: loving ourselves and each other, gaining wisdom, paying that wisdom forward, and improving our lives in the process. The outcome is not only transformational and sustainable, but through one-degree shifts, we will change this world that we created—together.

BeingTribal starts with you – what do you want your life to look like and feel like? It starts with changing your perspective to one of gratitude and being open to possibilities. I had to start waking up everyday in a state of gratitude and be grateful for what I had and who I wanted to become and all the glorious possibilities I was going to be manifesting through my thoughts, words, and deeds.

So, what helped me stay positive each day?

1. I wake up and think about what I am grateful for. Before I even open my eyes or look at my phone or talk to anyone, I think about what I am grateful for.
2. When I'm out in the world, when I walk by people, I like to look them in the eyes and wish them a good morning or good evening as I smile. Sharing just a little compassion and kindness makes me happier. I smile even when I don't want to because it will eventually make me smile authentically.
3. At work, I check in with my work tribe. At home, I check in with my family tribe, and so on.

4. I remember that everything is possible. I don't see my failures as mistakes or errors, I see my mistakes as opportunities to gain wisdom and I give myself grace.

I know this may sound like I am taking some kind of mood-altering substance, but I try everyday to feel happy, to connect with others and see the possibility. Does that mean that I am perfectly happy everyday? NOPE! There are times that I wake up and I create an instant list of what I didn't do, should have done, and what I did wrong. This train of thought, I quickly interrupt, and end my ride on the no-where train. I am so incredibly imperfect that I have bathed in my burdens and grumpiness until my fingertips resemble a prune, like a kid who spent too much time in a swimming pool. Then I catch myself and *"turn my frown upside-down"* – by the way, my kids hate when I say that – and focus on gratitude and start over again.

30

Have you ever heard of kintsukuroi? There is an art form in Japan called *kintsukuroi,* which means "to repair with gold." When a ceramic pot or bowl would break, the artist would mend the piece with gold or silver lacquer, actually making it stronger and more beautiful than before. The scars of the break are not something to hide because the bowl or pot is now more valuable because of its damaged history. I am beautifully broken and remade whole by my past and am more beautiful and wiser than ever. Kintsukuroi is an example of living that embraces every flaw and imperfection. Every crack is part of the past that I believe carries wisdom with it. We are more beautiful, precisely because we have been broken.

I remind myself that I am beautifully broken and made whole by the peace, compassion, abundance, and grace around me. That life has so much adventure ahead and with every new crack will come more GOLD! I will be more beautiful along the way.

Chapter Three

WHY BEINGTRIBAL?

"The best kind of people are the ones that come into your life and make you see the sun where you once saw clouds. The people that believe in you so much, you start to believe in you, too. The people that love you, simply for being you. The once in a lifetime kind of people."

— *Unknown*

Several years ago, I was in a tribe, long before I even knew what a tribe was. Our group of devoted friends was sitting around a kitchen table together. Our friend Susan (not her real name) was going through a divorce. She wore perfectly matched tennis shorts and shirt. We loved Susan, because she was the "fitness" queen of our group. Susan was beautiful. Her long brown hair was pulled back in a neat ponytail. She always looked put together. She was physically fit, toned and tanned, and she was as successful as she was beautiful... *and* she was broken.

We only knew she felt broken because she told us. From the outside, anyone would think she had everything, but they would have been wrong. Susan was in the lowest place she thought she could be. She was carrying the burden of her described failure. Failure to her children, her family, her faith... it was her ownership of shame and guilt that left her broken. There were five of us there. We were in a sun-lit kitchen and we were there because we all responded to the call "I need help" from Susan. Which, by the way, takes great courage for anyone to say! The "I can't do this anymore" kind of trouble. We sat around the table and listened as Susan slowly shared her grief. We listened, and we cried together, and then, we tried to fix it for her, giving her suggestions and advice. She politely nodded, and we were firmly planted in the problem-solving mode.

That is when wisdom stepped in and one of our friends interrupted us. Julie, simply said, "Stop it." We all looked up at her, a bit shocked, and she repeated it again. "Stop talking and stop trying to fix it." She was allowed. She was in her third recurrence of breast cancer and Julie had been through hell and back. She put her hands over Susan's and looked her right in the eyes and asked, "What is your biggest fear?" Susan wasn't sure how to answer and Julie repeated, "It's okay; what is your biggest fear?" And like a flood of words, Susan began to share her fears. One by one, sharing these huge fears, (failing marriage, losing her children, losing herself, her identify, having no future, being homeless) and it became uncomfortable and scary for me personally, because I had the exact same fears. I could tell from the looks around the room that we all shared some or all of those fears. Intently listening, Julie said, "Okay, those really are the worst it could get." She then asked, "If you were to pick the very worst of them all, what is the chance that it would really happen?"

Susan kind of laughed, blew her nose and said, "Not very likely." Julie continued down the list until the most probable fears were ones she was already dealing with.

Julie said, "Sometimes you have to take the fear monster out of your head. You have to look it straight in the eyes and tell it there is no room for it to exist in your world." One of us joked, "Unless it's the cookie monster," and it was in that moment that the air, thick with grief and fear dissipated and the light was brighter than before.

Julie changed our lives in that moment. She said that it was an exercise that she learned from another patient who was also receiving cancer treatment. Julie said, "In life, you have to walk into and through the pain. You have to lean into it, so you can move past it. If you avoid the pain and grief, if you don't deal with it, you will never get past it. It will never get smaller in your heart. You need to dissolve the pain through the process of living through it. Then and only then will it create space for new energy. New love."

Big tears filled my eyes. We all began to cry because we had all felt the pain of loss. We were all there in that moment to heal. I learned that day that every moment creates a mirror into your own life. It allows you to be witness to your own journey and be present in it.

Julie challenged Susan and all of us to recognize and embrace moments like these in our lives. In other words, when you feel like there is no light ahead, it's time to stop and pay attention. Take notice of it and do not fear it. She spoke about how being at our worst feels like we are vacant of hope in some way, and we are listening for any hope or relief. She said, this is when God or Spirit speaks to us through other people.

I truly believe that when we journey through new doors, we gain wisdom and appreciation for making it through the pain. How we recover from it is where life's wisdoms live. We then have the obligation to share the wisdom of the journey to pay it forward.

Julie continued, "I am dying of cancer. I will most likely never see my children have children. I will never grow old and sit around with my friends and tell stories. But I know that I can sit with you all now and tell you that you are going to get through this because you can pay attention to this moment. In this moment you are surrounded by unconditional love and you are strong enough to survive this." Julie reached across the table and held Susan's hands and we all grabbed their hands and cried. I watched this beautiful moment between two amazing women suddenly change all of us.

This is the perfect example in the simplest form of why BeingTribal is dearly needed. We need our closest people around us to be our trustworthy confidants. We can trust that they will lift us up and we will lift them up. Through this, we can walk through any doorway to wisdom and possibility. Sometimes, BeingTribal is just reminding each other to pay attention to the moments of our life, so we can believe in our own journey.

Susan and Julie, along with the other women there that day, helped me transform into the woman I am today. Because I learned to pay attention and lean into my grief. This beautifully broken woman made whole by love and wisdom and the belief that if I pay attention when life isn't easy, I can see the light that is ahead and know each journey has a purpose far larger than my own experience. They taught me the importance of giving grace to myself and others.

We all make mistakes or find ourselves in seemingly unbearable situations. Never forget the power of your tribe to lift you up, provide you with peace, compassion, abundance, and grace in the most authentic way. Your tribe will show you lit doorways to walk through, just as you will do for them. Have the reciprocal love affair with the possibilities of what your life could look like, and feel how it will impact others.

In the end, it is all about surrounding yourself with people who empower you to slowly become the person you are meant to be. Transformation takes time and it's so important to give yourself grace to respect and move through the process of change, one-degree shifts at a time.

Maya Angelou wrote, "You may encounter many defeats, but you may not be defeated. In fact, it may be necessary to encounter the defeats, so you can know who you are, what you can rise from, how you can still come out of it."

My favorite part of transformation is the gratitude you have for yourself when you walk through a door and make it through the journey, and the gratitude for the new

36

wisdom you can now pay forward. That is purposeful. The wisdom you gain is meant to pass through you to help guide others.

I have work tribes and my family tribe – for my personal tribes, I chose to have women-only tribes because I felt safe in that space. I wanted to be able to share my thoughts, fears, hopes, and dreams with people who lifted me up. For me, that has always been female energy. No judgment—just support. The ability to have complete trust and honesty with each other was a requirement and still is today in any successful tribe. These women who I knew and know today have my back and I have theirs. Confidences are held, and no masks are worn. We can be vulnerable to each other and know that what we talk about in our tribe stays in our tribe.

There is another higher purpose to BeingTribal. It is in the collective calling to elevate the positive energy to make a difference. Transformation of our individual lives, our tribe, spilling out to our community and ultimately the world.

Jane Fonda said, "Female friendships are just a hop to our sisterhood, and sisterhood can be a very powerful force."

So why do I believe in BeingTribal? Because, we need trusted people to thrive in life. We need authentic relationships and perspectives to guide us. Like keeping a puck in play on an air-hockey table. Its sounds harsh but you get bounced around in life and it is so much better to have those you trust be blunt and honest then be falsely gentle and placate a bad decision. We are animals and in nature the world is harsh sometimes. We have the ability to live amazing lives, and empower and lift up others to create a beautiful world. So, we need to surround ourselves with compassionate and authentic people.

Margaret Paul, Ph.D. wrote, "Humans, like many other animals, need each other. We are social beings and we are not meant to be alone." She went on to say, "We thrive when we feel connected and supported by each other, and we suffer when connection and support are not available. We have these needs as babies and we never lose them." When two or more people find common ground, they can connect authentically and see a pathway to a meaningful relationship. In a meaningful relationship, a door to compassion, trust, love and the exchange of wisdom manifests. This type of relationship can change your perspective or lens of the world. That new lens or view of the world happens in this simple exchange of wisdom and connection.

I need authenticity and purposeful relationships in my life. I crave it. The kind of relationship, outside of a romantic one, where I can connect with others to share passions for life and see how we can not only improve our own lives but pay it forward. It is such a powerful connection and I can literally feel the electricity charge the room.

Being with your tribe must be a trusted place where you can be vulnerable without wearing masks, and be honest about what you want your life to look like and feel like. It also allows you to find common ground with others who want the same journey. I think we are all craving this experience. I may be writing this book and sound wise from time to time, but that doesn't mean I haven't had moments when I felt like I had failed at being a wife or a mother or a friend. Locked in a bathroom, crying so hard that I didn't know what was tears, drool or snot. Life is not easy nor elegant, but it is an adventure to be reveled in with people who you know have your back and will wipe off your face and chin, and hug you even if your tears, snot, and drool are getting on them too.

I would not be where I am today without my tribes. I have come to truly believe that anything is possible because my tribes and I have a reciprocal love affair with the possibility of a more compassionate world to live in.

What Is BeingTribal?

There are various definitions of "tribe." The definition I prefer is from your dictionary.com: a group of people, or a community with similar values or interests, or a group with a common ancestor, or a common leader.

I have asked my tribe members how they would define a tribe. This is what they had to say: "BeingTribal is creating an authentic, purposeful, and trust-filled connection with other people." Another said, "BeingTribal is a kind of a movement or calling to reach out to others and do great things together to make a difference." A third person said, "I use my tribe to hold myself accountable and thrive in my life. I have learned so much and I like the idea of paying wisdom forward."

Asking yourself why you want BeingTribal aspects in your life is important. What do you want your life to look and feel like?

I know that every single member of every tribe I have been a part of has had wisdom to share and the inertia of that gained wisdom has changed my life in big and small ways. I learned to journal in a tribe. I learned to create vision boards in tribes. I learned to meditate and state my truth in a tribe. I learned to lose my fear around confrontation and be authentic in a tribe. I have learned to love myself in tribes, and trust me when I say that loving myself has been a huge journey for me.

I learned all these things and more because I learned them together with my tribe members. I figured out what worked for me. BeingTribal is not about all doing the same thing at the same time. It is about discovering who you are and bringing tools to the tribe to experience and try to see if this might work for one or more members and talk about it. It's about learning from each other. It's about practicing life slowly, in one-degree shifts. Now I journal every day and each year my children and I create vision boards of what we want in our lives. Some of the things I tried, I didn't like. For instance, I do not love running. I enjoy a 5K "jog" every once in a while, but I will never be a runner. I enjoy yoga and reiki, but I don't choose to eat vegan or be gluten-free.

Perfection is not the goal. Finding the right energy that you fit into *is*. I know that sounds a bit vague, but if you feel good around certain people, your energy melds with their energy.

40

This is one of the most common questions I receive from people, whether they are building a work tribe or personal tribe: "How do I choose my tribe?" It's a powerful question. Who you choose to be in your tribe or who is in a tribe you are considering joining is all about the energy of the people. The late business philosopher Jim Rohn said, "You are the average of the five people you spend the most time with." I believe wholeheartedly in this concept. Why? Because I have chosen the wrong people, for me, in the past. It happens. You may build a tribe and find out that you are not the right person for them. This is not a popularity contest. These are people that you authentically connect with and have common ground with.

How did I figure out they weren't the right fit? We didn't have the same core values or the same focus that I wanted to connect with. At first, I thought I should choose my tribes because they were *popular* or were in the right crowd or who I thought I wanted to emulate, only to discover that it was not a good emotional, physical or energetic fit for me. The relationship felt fake or they betrayed my confidence or I simply felt insecure around them. There are so many examples of how I have learned through the years who I wanted to be in my life. Once I tuned into my own body giving me signals, it rarely happens that I spend time with someone who isn't a good fit for me. We will discuss this more in the next section.

Everyone has an energy about them. Some people say it's an aura and others say it's an attitude. Either way, you should always want to surround yourself with people that you feel good around. This requires you to turn up all your senses.

In the chapter ahead, I list some ways to choose the right tribal members but there are a few things that I have learned over the years:

1. A tribe may last for a year or several years. We come in and out of each other's lives for reasons and that is perfectly fine. It's normal to be nomadic in our tribal relationships. People leave tribes, too, and that is okay.

2. Keep your promises to your tribe. If you promise to do something, do it. This is not so much about keeping your word to another person or group… it is about building your integrity. This also means keeping a promise to yourself. Don't promise something that isn't good for you. My grandfather always said, *you are only as good as your word.* When you create a track record of doing what you say you are going to do, you build self-trust and the trust of others and that is priceless.

3. Tell the truth. I work very hard each day to only say what I mean. People notice if you are full of shit… and boy in my past I have been a liar. Remember in the *foreword.* I learned to lie before I told the truth. Well, I had to retrain my brain to tell the truth. I don't have all the answers and I will tell the truth and people trust me because I only say what I believe and admit when I don't know the answer. This is another form of being only as good as your word.

4. Keep confidences like your life depends on it. When you promise to keep something confidential – do it. Don't ever use someone else's secret as a conversation

starter. Don't betray a friend or colleague to climb a personal or professional ladder. Be trustworthy and committed. How you live your life is karmic.

5. Don't judge or assume you wouldn't do something or act a certain way. You have not walked in that person's shoes. No one put you in charge of marshalling the sins of the world. You don't know what you don't know. Sit in compassion and empathy as you help a tribal member.

Chapter Four

HOW DO YOU BUILD YOUR TRIBE?

Surround yourself with people who add value to your life. Who challenge you to be greater than you were yesterday. Who sprinkle magic into your existence, just like you do to theirs. Life isn't meant to be done alone. Find your tribe, and journey freely and loyally together.

~ Alex Elle

First, please, oh please, take time with this. Allow your emotional intelligence—*how you feel around others, what your "gut" tells you*—to influence your decision-making as much or even more than your intellectual intelligence.

Your tribe may be people you haven't met yet, or people you already know. Whomever you choose, make it intentional. What I mean is, be thoughtful about who

44

you want in your tribe. Think about the type of personality or belief system you want in your tribe.

When I decided to write this book, I began purposefully cultivating a new tribe. I paid attention to how I felt when I was around other people. I listened to my inner voice when I met someone who I thought would be a logical choice and then sat with it for a while. I have to admit, more often than not, I chose people simply because I felt good around them. They had a certain energy that seemed to click with mine. The six tribe members I settled with all share my core values. They all strive to be authentic. They have a strong desire to make a difference, and they all were looking for a connection to other women whom they could trust.

I chose to only have women in my tribe. I knew I was going to talk about sex, trust, fear, menopause and other rather "uterine" topics and I didn't want to try to edit myself in my tribe. I thought I was being sexist at first by only choosing women, but it is not about what other people think or believe, it's what is right for me. Again, being self-full. Listen to what feels right to you and do that. Having all women in my tribe was right for me. I needed to have the female energy around me with no sexual energy interrupting my focus.

BeingTribal is for every human being who wants to create authentic tribes and move their life forward. If you are a man, you may want to only have men in your tribe. It doesn't matter what anyone else thinks – it is about what *feels* right to you, in your heart and soul. I coach work tribes that include both men and women and how they can be successful as team members. Build your tribe and if it feels right, you are on your way.

I am blessed to work with amazing individuals of all genders and have many friends of all genders whose councel I trust and respect. Two people can look alike but have a different mindset with different goals. I have seen a greater need for authentic communities of women supporting each other in the past few years than ever. Maybe, because as a woman, I want to change the culture of judgment and women competing and undermining each other, instead of women lifting each other up. You have the power to build your tribe with whomever you feel comfortable with. Do what is right for you.

As I mentioned before, I wanted to create a tribe who shared my core values. I wasn't sure if I knew what my core values actually were, so I wrote them down. I also wanted to look at what my life values were and what personality traits I wanted to be around. Again, I wrote those values and wants down because I needed to pay attention to what worked and didn't work for me.

I recommend you use a pencil for this exercise. It took me several tries to finalize my list. I also limited myself to five in each category. I wasn't shopping for groceries and I certainly am not perfect. I used these values as guidelines, not definite determiners.

Here are a few examples of core values: honesty, punctuality, integrity, trustworthy, frugality, spirituality.

How I determine what my most important values are is by determining how I felt about the opposing value.

For instance, being honest and authentic is very important to me. So is being financially responsible and being prompt. So, when I am off course—late, in debt, tell a lie—I feel bad about who I am as a person, and it causes me stress. That is an easy indicator of the value's importance. How you feel

46

about your behavior is your built-in value barometer. I also expect those values out of the people I have in my life.

1. Identify and write down what your **core values** are.

2. Now that you have identified your core values, write down your **life values**. Life values are more about how you live your life and what you are passionate about. Examples are: being just and fair, believing in equality, listening to others to learn not just to respond, being kind to others, standing up for what you believe even though it is not popular. Okay, okay, that is more of a mission statement but it is what I am passionate about. Write down your **life values**, what you are passionate about.

3. Finally, identify and write down the types of **personality traits** you enjoy being around and that work well for you. Examples are: people who tend to be optimistic, logical, artistic. I enjoy people and I respect those who offer their opinion when it differs from mine because I already know they have good intent. One of my dear friends used to say, "Some people's glasses are half empty, some people's glasses are half full, and some people just have broken glasses." I try not to hang out with people who choose to play "devil's advocate" or who derail progress. It pops my idea balloon. I like to think big and I truly believe that everything is possible! Write down the **personality traits** you want to be around.

This above exercise is critical because you need to find a group that you feel comfortable with. Once again, respect and trust are key! Being able to confide in each other and having complete confidentiality and commitment to respect each other's stories are two of the most important pieces. Do not join or cultivate a tribe that has someone you know is a gossip.

You may find that you already have your tribe and you are ready to dive in. You may need to cultivate or curate your tribe members.

One final reminder about building your tribe; build your tribe like a stone wall, not a brick wall.

What I mean by this is, make sure your tribe feels good to you and doesn't just look good to you. We spend so much time focused on how something looks and we forget to feel our way through life's decisions. Your tribe is a very important decision.

When I began focusing on purposefully building my tribe, I used all of my senses to manifest my tribe members. They were all people in my life, some longtime friends and others who I immediately connected with. I took the time, a little over two months, in fact. When I began asking people to be in my tribe, the time I took was important because we had already built relationships on respect and trust and they said yes. I invited them all over to my home for a retreat and it was funny to see all of their reactions. Some had met each other before and some had never met and they were all different... and guess what? They were all the same because they shared core values and life values and each had chemistry in their personality traits. It was so lovely to see how we all connected.

If you feel like you already have your tribe together, please still do the exercises in this chapter. This will help you logically and emotionally confirm that your tribe is complete. I prefer between four and eight members in a tribe. That number works for me. That does not mean you can't have a larger tribe. Your tribe will ebb and flow over time. Surround yourself with the right people from the beginning.

Please remember that this tribe is who you are going to begin your journey with. It will influence how you begin to shine as you celebrate yourself and each other and begin to practice life in one-degree shifts. Be selective! Human beings have a fundamental need to be felt, seen, and heard. Make sure you have the right people around you.

Here is another tool to identify the people that you might want to invite into your tribe. Remember to turn up all your senses! I cannot stress this enough. Use your emotional barometer to feel a person's energy and listen to and trust your gut. This is not a popularity contest. If you don't honor the process of cultivating your tribe, you will have false starts and challenges along the way.

The following exercise empowers you to create a list of people and divide them in two sections:

Make a List	
People in your life that lift you up, and you feel good when you are around them.	People in your life that make you feel uncomfortable or judged.

In the left column, list people in your life who you want to be in your life. You go to them with great news and they celebrate it with you and ask how they can help you find new ways to grow because they are always growing too. You are energized by them. They provide you wisdom and help you in problem-solving situations. In general, they lift you up.

In the right column, list people in your life that who have to be in your life – they are your family, co-workers or certain family friends. Whenever you talk to them about your life, they don't always bring positive energy to you. Rather, they sometimes provide negative feedback, or they are usually in some cycle of crisis. They are not the people you go to when you want to receive validation or wisdom.

Take inventory of who is in your left and right columns. Your tribe members could be some of the people in your left column.

Now, I'm going to ask you to be brave and honest with yourself. When there are people who want to be in your tribe and who are in your right column, please, oh please, remember that you are working to transform your life. I would not even tell people that you are selecting your tribe. Blame it on me and say, "Rena said that I can't have siblings or family members, co-workers or 'whomever' in my tribe."

Another way of looking at it is: this is your life, not a birthday party invitation. Be honest and kind. When someone wants to be in your tribe and they are not a good fit or worse, you know they are toxic or judgmental, do not invite them into your tribe. You are dedicating your time and energy to this tribe. This is a precious process and these are precious relationships. Do not allow people in your tribe who drain your energy. Remember to say "no" so you can make room to say "yes." Being honest and vulnerable takes courage. It doesn't happen overnight, it takes time. Celebrate your journey and love yourself for the person you have become and are still becoming.

The Invitation to Dance...

How do you invite someone into your tribe? I worked hard to pay attention to my process so I could share it with you. It was like sharing a recipe that you have cooked a hundred times and then trying to teach someone. When I began the tribe that helped me write this book, I told them all what I was doing.

I asked each of them to focus on what they wanted their life to look like and feel like and how we could empower each other to create that in a group. I authentically told each of them how I felt connected to them in some way. I even shared the moment I connected with them during a conversation. What I loved about this step was each of them knew exactly what moment I was talking about. I was 100 percent transparent because I needed to figure out what worked and did not work.

I then explained that I was going to hold a five-hour retreat and I asked them to be in my tribe. Each of them agreed and when we met we followed an agenda that can be found online at beingtribal.com.

Following that meeting, we set up a private Facebook Messenger page, where we could communicate, and we met every month for two hours, with as-needed check-ins in a private chat group. Each meeting we followed the same format (I will discuss this in the next chapter).

From the first gathering, it was magic. Every invited member had guilt-free, shame-free permission to say no to BeingTribal. It was important that we all could accept or decline the offer to be in the tribe after our first session. Having people that wanted and could commit to the tribe and to moving their lives forward was required.

There were many things I learned with this process:

1. This tribe worked for about six months but we all became very close friends. The tribe served the purpose of understanding that when you create a tribe, every person needs to be ready to make changes in their life and be transparent in their

struggles. Most of these tribal members went out to create their own unique tribes.

2. It is best to have a topic to focus on each month and to discuss. The topics are chosen by the tribe but some topics need more than a month to get through. For example, it may be a focus on money and budgeting for a month or two before you launch into diet and exercise. Each one-degree shift needs a month to fully implement. I compare it to the song the 12 Days of Christmas, where the gifts add on to each other.

3. It's okay for people to choose not to join a tribe. They may not feel safe or comfortable in the group.

4. Each tribal member needs to dedicate an hour every two weeks or two hours a month for a tribal meeting. If this journey is not important to them, then they just are not ready to be in a tribe.

5. There are occasions when a tribal meeting is not focused on a subject. For example, after the 2016 Presidential Election, we just all needed to get together, talk, cry, laugh, feel the fear of change and lean in to it. We then regrouped at the next meeting.

6. Perfection is not the goal. Yes, we want to change our lives for the better and we need to give ourselves time to make those changes. Life will throw curve balls at you and bring you to your knees. That is when you find your greatest wisdom. Love yourself first and believe that every experience has wisdom in it.

Chapter Five

TRIBAL GROUND RULES

*Be the reason someone smiles. Be the reason someone
feels loved and believe in the goodness in people.*

~ Roy T. Bennett

The next step was to set tribal commitments of behavior. As a tribe we set these commitments at our first monthly meeting. We created commitments to each other and to the tribe:

- Cell phones turned off and put away, out of sight
- One person talks at a time
- Respectfully focus on the member talking
- Positive sharing
- Complete confidentiality
- Be prompt to meetings
- Assign a timekeeper
- Each member has five minutes to speak

- Close the meeting with each tribal member providing a short positive intention.

There are several tools each tribal member should have. A notebook (three ring binder) is best, so you can add pages and educational materials you want to share or you receive in the tribe. You should also have a journal to write in each day. I have used lined journals and unlined journals. I write, draw, paste pictures in mine. I have found when you document your journey, you discover the progress you have made and it also allows for great insight into why we make the choices we make. There is a whole chapter about journaling later in this book. Buy a journal and a great pen to write with. A glue stick or tape may also prove beneficial, to add images, poems, etc., into your journey. Keep a list of affirmations in your binder or your journal. I like to reference my affirmations before and after my tribal meetings, especially since I often share or add to my list. Finally, I keep a copy of my vision board in my binder or journal. I have even kept a picture of my vision board on my phone. It allows me to continue to manifest what I want my life to look like and feel like.

These are all powerful tools and I encourage you to invest the time, money (doesn't have to be much) and energy into these tools. They keep you on track and accountable to yourself and your tribe.

Tribal meetings should always be held in a place with privacy. If possible, you might try rotating to each other's homes. Make it fair for everyone. Do not try to impress each other by the special treats you bring or by 'upping your game' to impress your tribe. The more down to earth you are, the more comfortable everyone will be. Make this process precious and worthy of the energy everyone is putting into it. Hold each other accountable. Use positive language when speaking to each other and *always* be honest. It protects the authenticity of the tribe. Bring water and tissues – they are always needed.

Keep all tribal communication off social media unless it's a private group and privacy is ensured. Your tribal progress is not a brag or a status update. This is a precious sacred process—honor it!

When you meet, these are the questions each tribal member will answer:

1. What am I working on?
2. What has been my biggest success?
3. What has been my biggest challenge?
4. What is a measurable goal I want to achieve in the next 30 days and how my goal can be met when I _____? (Remember, one-degree shifts or baby steps!)
5. The tribe will ask how they can help each member with the biggest challenge and any goal they are working toward.

Finally, take your tribal work seriously. This is transformational work and to be effective, you need to dedicate time during each week and before meetings. This is not about being perfect; this is about a journey to celebrate you and your tribe. You will share the wisdom of your journey to lift up your tribe. You will succeed and fail and that is part of the process.

You will learn more from your failures than your successes. Celebrate your courage in your journey. You will be amazed how your life can transform when you move in one-degree shifts.

Once we had our list of commitments, we each signed our names to the bottom of each copy and placed it in our notebooks. That was the beginning of the most empowering group I have ever been and continue to be a part of.

Remember to give yourself and others grace when the sticky sludge of life tries to derail your journey. It will happen. Pay attention to it. Walk through and keep moving forward. Share your experience with your tribe. Reach out to your tribe when the shit hits the fan and you need to cry or rant or just share your fears with the people who will listen and be present with you. Your awareness and reaction to these moments will change over time. When you look back at derailing moments, you will have a new perspective on your ability to cope and overcome challenges. Share that new wisdom with your tribe.

Elvis Has Left the Building...

Another question I am asked a lot is what if someone breaks the commitment of the tribe? How do we ask them to exit the tribe?

In all the tribes I have been honored to be a part of in the past, there has only been one time when a tribal member was asked to exit our tribe.

This was not a tribe that was cultivated; rather it was a group of friends that organically came together. We were always getting together and could talk about anything. It

58

was a heartbreaking experience because not only did it destroy our friendship, it took a whole year for our tribe to recover. One of our tribe members was asked to leave because she had personally betrayed another tribal member. I and another member were asked to have a very difficult but honest conversation with her. It took us all a long time to recover from that exit. It was painful and ultimately, the tribe didn't survive. We have all moved on and have fond memories of our friendships but it broke our trust and made us question our ability to "know" a person truly.

I share this with you because I believe betrayal of confidences is another reason why the thoughtful process of who you want to be in your tribe is very important and takes time. I need to know that I can trust the members of my tribe and so do you.

This story exemplifies why Tribal Commitments are so important. If you have mutually agreed on tribal ground rules and you each make a promise to honor them and each other, it is easier to discuss when a conflict or breach of confidence arises. It is very easy for a committed tribe to take on a "mean girl" mentality when an error in judgment happens. We are not perfect beings. In a cultivated tribe or an already existing tribe, with adopted commitments, the best way to handle exiting someone from the tribe is with honesty, compassion, and a chance to make things right.

1. It is best to talk about the situation openly and honestly in the tribe.
2. If the two tribal members cannot have a positive conversation directly then it is brought before the tribe. The assumption must be of good intent.

Whatever breach of commitment took place, it was a mistake.

3. I read somewhere that it is better to hold hands when you are talking about a problem because it allows compassion to enter the conversation. It has certainly worked in other experiences when I have coached a tribe through a challenge. So, if possible, have everyone hold hands.

4. Share the situation with the tribe, each member involved having their time to share. It is important to identify the feelings that are being felt. I feel betrayed, I feel hurt, I feel my trust with you is damaged. This needs to happen on both sides equally. When there is pain in a group, you must meet the group where they are and walk them out of the muck of that pain.

5. Ask what happened and what would each personally do differently if they could, and how they want to make this situation right. Ask the person who feels hurt to honestly listen to the member they feel betrayed by and ask if they can honor those words to move the tribe forward.

6. If a resolution is met, then you readdress your commitment statement. If a resolution is not met or it is not the first time this tribal member has broken the commitment, then you ask them to leave. I always think it is a great idea to have each member write down what good things they wish for the departing member and thank them for being part of the tribe.

I must share that it is rare that a tribal member is asked to leave for negative reasons. Usually someone is moving away or taking time out for other personal reasons.

If you have been asked to join a tribe, it is just as important to go to the initial meeting and have the four to five hours of connection to make sure this is the right group to commit to. Trust your emotional energy barometer and your gut during this time. Turn up your senses to ensure you are ready to join the tribe.

As I mentioned before on the tools I bring to my tribal meetings, this really is a life practice. The tools below have transformed my life. I will go in depth on each in the chapters ahead.

1. Positive Affirmations
2. Meditation
3. Journaling
4. Vision Boards
5. Creating a Personal Vision Statement.

Now, before your mind begins listing the reasons why this book has gone off the rails into la-la land, in the chapters ahead, I will share the science around all these practices and how they will manifest amazing results in your journey and your tribe. For now, you gotta trust me!

Well, you have made it this far into the book. Are you ready to create the life you have always wanted, and most importantly, love yourself throughout this process? Tall order, huh? Well, hang on, because we are going to create amazing energy together as you change your life, cultivate your tribe, and pay that wisdom forward!

Chapter Six

COMMON GROUND AND AFFIRMATIONS

"Your journey has molded you for your greater good. And it was exactly what it needed to be. Don't think that you've lost time. It took each and every situation you have encountered to bring you to the now. And now is right on time."

– Asha Tyson

I was getting ready for work one morning and I couldn't find the keys to my car. I began this internal rant of words that was so demeaning to myself. I literally stopped and thought, *I would never speak to anyone else like that. Why am I saying these things to myself?*

That day was a game changer for me and I began to do research on negative self-talk. Why do we all have negative self-talk or old tapes playing in our heads? It was like a Top 40 playlist of all the negative messages I have held onto

62

since I was a child. I received those messages that others said or that I perceived their reactions to be. Whether it was a parent, teacher, friend, lover, etc. As humans, we take it all in and turn up the negative interpretation of each message.

Why is it that our egos, replaying these negative messages, can bring us to our knees? I was done with beating myself up, because I knew if I wanted to change my life, I had to start with my own inner negative tapes. Just like everything else, I did it in one-degree shifts.

I sat in my meditation space and began to visualize a room in my head. A boardroom where all the negative voices came from. I imagined each of my negative old messages as individual, silly-looking puppets, like the creatures from the movie *Labyrinth*. I asked myself how something so juvenile and silly-looking could have any wisdom. I told myself that they couldn't because they weren't real. Slowly, those old tapes stopped playing. Whenever I began hearing those messages, I simply visualized going into my mind and walking up to the boardroom and slamming the door. Then, I found an even better answer: I replaced those old messages with positive messages and I created affirmations to post around my room, by my desk, at work, in my journal, and on my vision board. It was my personal way of reminding myself of my worthiness.

One day, I was sharing this with my dad. He said something pretty revealing. Now I preface this with the fact that my dad has over 30 years clean and sober, so he has known his own torments in life. He said, "I try not to spend time in my head because it is a very dangerous neighborhood." It made me laugh and then I realized he was so wise. I hold on to that wisdom to this day. We can create very toxic and destructive thoughts in our heads. It can be a very dangerous environment if we allow it to be.

There are many tools out there to change your negative self-talk. They will help you diminish those voices of doubt and negativity and help you find your own way to discount the credibility of those messages. I've included some tools in this chapter and others can be found on our website. You will also learn some great tips from your tribe.

How do you start? By throwing away your negative messages and replacing them with positive ones. It may sound simple and it can be...it also takes practice.

Beginning with easy and simple affirmations, you will learn to love yourself and embrace your own beauty and the beauty of those around you. Your tribe is there to support you as much as you are for them in this journey. Together, you will create a shared wisdom to lift each other up so you may pay it forward to help others do the same.

I call this chapter Common Ground and Affirmations because part of replacing the negative tapes with positive ones is also rooted in the fact that we are all the same. We all share a common human existence. The English Language Learners dictionary defines Common Ground as "something that people agree about even if they disagree about other things."

We don't have to agree about every aspect in our lives to have common ground. In fact, our world would be stagnant if we all agreed on every area. This most important perspective of common ground relates to feeling equally worthy.

We Are Human

We are all human beings who have each experienced the same feelings. The challenge comes when we allow society's standards, bigotry, and hate to disrupt our true belief that we are deserving of peace, compassion, abundance, and grace. Our human nature, our egos, drive us to measure ourselves against others. Are we more or less worthy than our neighbors?

Inevitably, we find ourselves falling short of what we believe we should be in our life. Why? We are telling ourselves the greatest lie ever told—that we are not good enough or worthy enough. We are just as worthy as anyone else on this planet. We are worthy of having our lives filled to the brim with love and compassion.

The Self-Lie

We are aided in this self-lie by our society (which we designed) telling us to compare our weight, income, race, marital status, sexual orientation, spiritual beliefs, and so on, to everyone else's. We, the human race, have designed our society to create condescending self-talk and we will need to transform it one person at a time, one tribe at a time, one community at a time, and so on.

The Urge to Compare

Too often we compare our lives to another's and discount our own feelings of worthiness. On the flip side of that, have you ever thought that your friend or neighbor has it easier in life than you do? And do you hold resentment or jealousy in your heart?

65

My sister once said to me, "I try not to judge my insides by someone else's outsides. You don't know what their true world looks like. We are all good at hiding our internal storms."

You Are Worthy

You are beautifully you in every way, exactly the way you are! Do you want to make changes in your life? Of course you do. We all do. First you must know in your heart, mind and soul that you are worthy! It is actually your human responsibility to feel worthy. You must capture it and hold it close. It must be the intent of equity that is held high as an integral part of your tribe. This is our common ground.

A tool I use in coaching tribes in order to find their common ground is to develop the skill to rewrite some of our negative self-talk.

Here is the exercise:

On a piece of paper, divide your paper in half with a line. At the top of the page, write down what negative messages or self-talk you hear in your head. What holds you back from becoming the "you" you are meant to be?

On the bottom half of the page, create a positive statement to each of the items above the line.

Example: the top part of the paper says, "I am overweight because I emotionally eat. The bottom statement might be, "I nurture my body by eating healthy whole foods."

There are steps to this exercise. 1. List the negative thoughts that have been streaming on your playlist and you believe have held you back. 2. Replace those old discredited messages with new affirmations. Not only will it change your energy when you focus on your positive messages, over time you won't even give energy to the negative noise that used to play such a suffocating role in your life.

It was very helpful for me to identify where my old tapes came from, clarify or invalidate them, and then modify or change them into positives.

When you consider that many of those old messages looping in your head can stop you in your tracks, it is important to recognize them and recode your brain to think differently in all of these areas.

Identify – Clarify – Modify

1. Take time to write the old messages down and identify what the root of the feeling is and where you think it first developed.
2. Clarify why you think you have held onto it for so long and see the falsehood of the lie you have been telling yourself by identifying your strengths.
3. Recode your thinking by modifying your old messages. Write the new messages with positive language. Solidify them with positive words and sentences.
4. Do this for as many messages as you need to, inserting extra journal pages as needed. Use large font for positive messages and smaller font for negative messages. Try gluing images from magazines or online sources on your pages. Those images you begin to create will also translate to your vision board.

One of my ways to encode these positive thoughts or affirmations in my life is to write them on sticky notes. I was so desperate to start this process, no sticky notes on hand, I used lipstick and eyebrow pencil to write these simple affirmations on my bathroom mirror. They were replaced soon after with dry erase marker and I still do it this to this day.

Identify: Write the negative thoughts.

Clarify: Where did they come from?

Modify: Replace with positive affirmations.

Release the Old Tapes

When you and your tribe meet next, take out your folded piece of paper with those old negative messages on it. Use wish paper that you can buy online, on beingtribal.com or even burn regular paper in a safe metal garbage can. I like "wish paper" because when you light it, it floats up into ash and it seems symbolic to me to turn negative thoughts into disappearing ash. So, write down those messages, and when you burn them, allow it to become a release of those negative thoughts and energy from your mind and body. Allow it to make room for the positive thoughts you are creating.

I like to write down my negative thoughts on the wish paper and crumple it up in my hand to begin to destroy those thoughts. In order for the wish paper to work, you now flatten out your wish paper, roll it into a tube. This is a great exercise to do with your tribe. Have each of your tribal members bring their wish paper and stand in a circle. One by one, light your wish paper on fire. The paper will burn quickly into ash as it floats to the sky. You can either let it float away or catch it with your hands and rub the ash between your hands until it disappears.

Think to yourself or say out loud, "I release you!"

You are allowing these positive messages to be your new Top 40 playlist. You own your self-talk and it will transform you. Like any practice in life, it will take time. Please be patient with yourself.

Celebrate with your tribe. Laugh, giggle, dance, sing, and enjoy this moment. You are transforming your life!

I love to do this exercise with my work team at the end of each year when we set goals. We list our biggest failures and what we learned from them. We keep this wisdom that we learned and burn the failure. The whole purpose of failure is to gain wisdom. I love when I fail because 1. I tried something new and learned what didn't work and 2. I found how to make it work and in turn can share whatever wisdom I learned. It is awesome!

What has helped me.

1. Practice your affirmations and have them in more than one place; in the bathroom, in your bedroom, in your office, in your journal, in your car, on your phone – wherever you may need to access them.
2. Treat every person as you want to be treated – with respect, compassion and kindness.
3. Give yourself grace and take time to see the wisdom from your mistakes.
4. Be gentle with yourself. Love your body, mind and soul.

If you want to see a list of affirmations, check out our website for free downloadable worksheets.

Delight in this celebration of transformation!

70

Chapter Seven

MEDITATION, FAITH, AND GRATITUDE

"Prayer is you speaking to God. Meditation is allowing the spirit to speak to you."

– Deepak Chopra

This is one of my favorite topics because I am always trying to see new pathways to my higher self and my true intention for what my next steps will be in life.

My grandmother was both Chinook Indian and French. She was a devoted Catholic and she faithfully meditated on her rosary everyday. I say meditation because that was what it was like. You didn't disturb her when she was praying. She also had visions that meant different things to her. For instance, she told me once that when she has a vision of a man standing in a doorway with a cane, that meant someone close to her was going to pass on.

71

Grandma Pearl used to share such powerful statements about how the past can teach us yet doesn't define us. She had incredible wisdom and the quote below is one of my favorite:

> "Those who pass before us, sit upon our shoulders and whisper life's truths, so we may have a wiser journey, until we become the whisperers."
>
> ~Pearl Thom.

I learned as I grew older that she meant angels and spirit guides and I know she is still guiding me to this day.

For me, prayer is sitting in gratitude to God, the universe, my spirit guides, and they support me with their enduring love and wisdom. I see meditation as receiving wisdom from a higher energy vibration where I believe all positive love and light exist. I start my day by checking in with my spirit guides and ask them for guidance and light.

I calm my mind and body and simply receive by focusing on my breath and I go to one of my sacred places in my mind. Remember when you were a child and you would play pretend games? Well, I rely on that same ability to just be in one of my sacred places. I imagine myself walking into the garden that my grandfather planted when I was a child—that is where I seek wisdom from God, my angels and spirit guides. I can ask them questions, I can ask for energy or direction, and sometimes I just need to feel loved, so I can use that beautiful energy throughout my day.

This is my way of resetting my mind and body from stress and disruptive thoughts, and opening new space for wisdom, love, and light.

I had an amazing mentor in my grandmother. I believe she had great wisdom as she connected through meditation and prayer to God, angels and her past loved ones. She was so insightful for the generation she was born into. As a young woman, she dealt with bigotry through both her faith and her race, yet she was steadfast in her belief of standing up for her beliefs. She taught me to always stand up for those who don't have a voice and equal rights. She was a devout Catholic but believed what a woman does with her body is between her and God, and when two people love each other, their gender does not matter, and we must remember that "God" is the foundation of love and compassion.

She affected our entire family through her wisdom and candor. She would speak out, even when her ideas were unpopular, if she thought someone's rights were being oppressed. I believe that her meditation and prayer, her connection to a higher power, enabled and empowered her courage to be so convicted in her beliefs. Her meditation and prayer grounded her in life and allowed her to speak her truth. I wanted so badly to be as brave as she was. It was why I worked on my own relationship with God and the niverse. She is the reason why I meditate and pray and am grateful for the life I am able to lead.

The Benefits

There are thousands of studies proving meditation benefits your body by reducing stress and anxiety, as well as resetting your mind for greater clarity of thought and awareness. Did you know it also benefits your heart and nervous system? Taking time to intentionally meditate is critical to your whole health.

Starting my day off with meditation—even if it is only five minutes—allows me to connect to life at a higher level of consciousness. I am less stressed, I am calmer, and I manifest light and abundance into my life more easily.

Even though my grandmother was a master at prayer and meditation, I struggled with it. I couldn't get my mind out of the list-making mode. What worked for me was connecting first thing with my spirit guides. It didn't happen right away. I had to practice and fail and practice and study and try new things and I finally found two or three things that worked for me.

Meditation isn't just sitting in the lotus position, and chanting "ohm," at least not for me. I can take my consciousness to a higher level when I am cooking a favorite recipe. Sometimes, it is when I am prepping vegetables like shucking corn or snapping asparagus spears. I intentionally ask for light and love to surround me and wisdom to be received and I can connect in deeper thought.

We are all capable of channeling wisdom from God, our angels and spirit guides. It is just learning how to connect and listen to their "whispers" as my grandmother used to say.

Have you ever been talking with a friend who is having a difficult moment in time and suddenly you say something that is wise and profound, and it just seems to be the exact thing they needed to hear? And you think later, "Where did that come from?" Well, love and positive wisdom is channeled through us to help those around us. We are spirits in human form right now in this moment. Whether our wisdom comes from our past lives, from our angels and spirit guides, I don't know. I do know we need those "whispers" of wisdom to help ourselves and others move forward and heal through whatever we are experiencing. This is another form of connecting to your higher self to receive these wisdoms and it is all part of meditation.

Creating a healing space

Let's talk about how to set yourself up for success in learning to meditate in the most traditional manner. I personally do need a few things to be successful in meditation. I need to have a quiet, comfortable space in my home. Set aside a space in your home that is not used for anything else and make sure it is a defined space like the corner of your bedroom or an area that doesn't have any foot traffic. If you live alone, you can place it anywhere. Wherever it is, you want to honor it as your sacred space.

If you don't live alone, and especially if you have children, you will want to set some boundaries to ensure that your family understands how important this space is to you. Encourage your children to also have their own space in their rooms.

1. **Protect your sacred space.**

   Describe how you will protect this space from clutter and let everyone in your home know that this is your private sacred space.

75

2. Set a dedicated time.

Making time for your meditation to begin your day is great. You may choose to end your day with meditation. Commit to a time of day and write it down in the space below. Describe why you want to commit to this time.

3. Set a timer.

I learned early on that if I set a timer, I won't be thinking about how long or how short I have been meditating. I give away that worry or preoccupation to my wind-up timer or phone. Just be available to allow this time for you.

Describe below how you might remove other distractions from your meditation time.

4. Make it comfortable.

Add a cushion or two to this space. Place calming photos, quotes or poems in your space. I use guided meditation, so a space to place my phone or iPad is important.

Describe below what you want your sacred space to look and feel like.

5. Prepare for your meditation.

I preload guided meditations and music so when I prepare to center my mind and body, I am not scrambling for these resources. Spend time finding resources on meditation and write them below.

6. Seek out classes.

There are many community resources where you can learn to meditate. Find what works for you. Go to local meditation classes or watch guided meditation videos on YouTube. I have several listed on our website. Ask friends who you know meditate about their favorite practice. Write a list of resources in your community.

77

Remember that we are practicing life in one-degree shifts. Perfection is not the end goal, but finding time to love yourself and honor yourself is. Even if you start this process and only last a few minutes, give yourself credit for starting. I have several five-minute guided meditation videos on our website for you to experience with your tribe.

Finding a meditation style that works for you is important to begin each day. If and when my day is becoming stressful, I take a break to restore my energy with a quick meditation. There are several apps on your phone you can use for this purpose. Those are listed on our website as well.

I have been asked what faith I am. I always find this amusing because I simply have faith in God, the universe and all that is love.

At the beginning of this book I mentioned four beliefs that I hold dear:

1. Love is powerfully real, and it conquers hate every day!
2. Change can only start when you begin to love yourself more than anyone else.
3. We need each other.
4. Everything is possible.

I believe that love and faith are one and the same.

I encourage you to have faith in yourself first. You need to authentically believe you can do anything you set your mind to. All is possible with faith and love in yourself. I have seen miracles happen because of faith in a treatment and the love and support of people—prayer chains work! Why? Because our soulful selves are sending love and healing energy to one person and it is powerful. The connected energy and love transform us because we have faith that it is power, which manifests into healing energy, and the person receiving it believes that this healing energy will change an outcome. We have the power to heal ourselves and each other. That is not to say that we don't need modern medicine, because the discoveries we have made in medicine, both eastern and western, have been given to us to heal our world. It is the wisdom and love that we use to heal others that is all from the same source.

I truly have faith in God, the universe, and in the goodness of others. Even the basic belief in the "Golden Rule," to treat others as you wish to be treated, is a great example of having faith. I believe that good wins over evil and love lives in our hearts. I have faith in myself as a good, kind, loving person. I have faith that I am creating positive love and light for myself, my family, my tribe, my community, and the world.

When we are in the depths of despair, we seek out faith. I have witnessed the power of my mother's deep faith in God and Jesus Christ as her Lord and Savior. I celebrated her faith with her and knew it carried her through as she lost her battle with brain cancer. Her faith gave us all faith that she is now at home with God.

In my nearly two decades of working in healthcare, I have seen the power of prayer and good energy that have created miracles. I believe we need to have a connection to a higher power, to nature, to the universal energy or some other space that replenishes our hearts and souls and a true belief in goodness.

I also know deep in my heart that God and the universe will provide for me. I have faith that I will make good decisions and I will work to do the right thing, not for any other reason than to pay forward all the love and wisdom I have been honored to receive. I think our faith is what we rely on when we need to walk out of tragedy and pain into the light of day. The faith that tomorrow is going to be a better day.

I have used very general references to spirituality and religion in this book, because I respect all beliefs if they promote love and wisdom. Every teaching I have come across from our ancient texts has promoted the love and equality of one another. All degrading, *us versus them* doctrines are man's manipulation to what they want to portray in order to control others. It is a powerfully manipulative tool to say only this group is right. That is not true under any of God's teachings regardless of the religion you are referencing.

I wish for you great faith in yourself. Believe that you can do anything you set your mind to. Believe in and have faith in your tribe. Together we will change the world!

I wanted to end this chapter on gratitude. There are times when I am having a difficult day. An easy way to authentically *turn my frown upside down*, is to stop and think about or even say out loud what I am grateful for. It changes my energy level my heart feels warm, and my demeanor completely changes. It is even better when I share with someone why I am grateful for them in my life.

Emitting personal gratitude will not only make their day, but it will turn up your own positive energy! Stop what you are doing, take a walk outside and look at this beautiful world we live in. Be grateful for your mind and your ability to think. Be grateful for your free will and your ability to choose to be kind and loving. Be grateful for whatever you can find, small or large. I am grateful that I have food to eat everyday and healthy children and all my fingers and toes. I am incredibly grateful for all the moments of my childhood and adolescence, no matter how painful because I have wisdom that I would never have had otherwise.

Be grateful for the lessons learned. They truly help us to transform as a soulful person, and that surely is something to be grateful for. When someone tells me that they have made a mistake, I share with them how awesome it is that the mistake happened, because we don't learn a lot when we win, or when everything is easy. We learn when we make mistakes.

Write down five things you are grateful for and make sure you share with the people who helped create those "things" in your life. It will not only change your day, it will truly change theirs as well.

What has helped me meditate, have faith, and be grateful:

1. I got into meditation because it was the only way to quiet my mind from the racing, ranting, and self-deprecating thoughts of my childhood. Meditation

81

was recommended to me by a counselor. I went to energy healing sessions, meditation classes, reiki sessions. I asked everyone I knew who meditated how they did it. I bought books and tapes and audio downloads, and I logged onto YouTube and watched videos. I found what worked for me. It wasn't what worked for some of my friends. Try and practice and try some more. Find what works for you and keep it simple.

2. Being in healthcare as long as I have, I have seen medical tragedies and I have seen miracles. I have seen someone with little chance of survival be surrounded in healing energy and prayer and the power of faith that all things are possible, change the outcome of a patient. Faith is believing in what is not in front of you, and I now, in this time in my life, know that faith is incredibly powerful. When you believe in the possibility of magic and manifestation, you give it real energy to show up in your life and the lives of those around you. Have faith that all things are possible, because I am here to tell you that they are.

3. Waking up every morning with gratitude has changed my life. When I am fearful or nervous, it is my go-to energy changer. It's the magic pill for sitting in worry. Being grateful and sharing your gratitude changes everything. It changes your mindset, your ability to manifest, and the energy around you.

Chapter Eight

WEAVING YOUR FABRIC

"Life is the weaving together of moments and events over time. It moves even when we are stuck in the past or fearful of the future. Until we can learn to know us, to accept us and be happy with us, how can we ever expect to be happy with anyone else? Too often we seem fixed on the idea that happiness comes from others or from the attainment of things. In reality happiness comes from making peace with our mistakes, wanting to know who we are and what we want in life and understanding being alone doesn't mean being lonely."

– Jane Changes

You are who you choose to be. A friend of mine told me once when I was dealing with a great sadness, you *choose your scar*. When you are in a moment in life when your heart is broken you choose whether this event will leave you with a "d" for defeat or a "v" for victory. It made so much sense to me because

83

when we have loss or sadness in our life, this is when we learn the most. We don't learn volumes of knowledge when everything is sunny.

Years ago, I made the decision to turn my childhood trauma of abuse into wisdom. It was keeping me locked up in a cage of guilt and shame. It took me a very long time to recognize that my experiences were not who I was, but part of the fabric of my life. It was my wisdom and strength. We have all been betrayed. It is another part of our common ground. We have also been loved and felt joy. Our life experiences make up our fabric, which will continue to weave as we live our life. Each profound experience in our lives has a great purpose. It gives us perspective for gratitude and understanding of the journey that we have made, and it helps inform us of how we view the journey ahead. Our wisdom informs our love and compassion, our ability to decide what we want life to look like, and even who we want in it. All of your life experiences have created who you are today.

I was in my mid-twenties when I knew I was in danger of losing myself completely to an endless, muted, gray life. I had two ways to go about changing my life and getting out of the muck I felt trapped in. 1. I could have tried to find help through only my faith, which was suggested by my pastor. He suggested that if I prayed and had a strong enough faith that God would show me the way to healing. Or 2. Seek serious professional counseling that was based on science and process. I chose to seek out therapy while acknowledging the role that my meditation, faith, and prayer played in my healing. So, I got help. I went to someone I could trust and knew would be honest with me. They suggested a counselor who was progressive. I look back now and I realize it took great courage for me to seek out what I wanted and not just do what I was told. I believe my angels and spirit guides were showing me the way.

By the grace of God, I found a professional who gave me advice. He told me not to sit around in a circle and talk about the shit that happened and relive it over and over again. I'm telling you *don't do that!* It's not *still* happening to you! You need to find a light out of this tunnel.

He referred me to another wonderful counselor and she gave me life-changing tools. The most powerful was what I called "my theater." She asked me to close my eyes and envision I was in a large dark room that was mine, and I was safe, and in charge. It was my own movie theatre and in front of me was a giant movie screen. My theatre and no one else's. I owned it. I was in control.

I was having anxiety attacks and flashbacks of the sexual abuse—painful moments, tastes and smells—I couldn't escape them. My counselor taught me to place each of these flashbacks on my movie screen. In my pocket was my hammer. It seemed giant to me. It was light to my touch yet powerful to possess. When I would have a flashback that overwhelmed me, I would put that image, smell or taste up on my screen and I would visualize myself throwing my powerful hammer at my movie screen, shattering the memory like glass into a million tiny pieces and watch it disintegrate. Amazingly, over time, I stopped having panic attacks. Eventually, I didn't have those flashbacks at all. I owned my world and I was in control, not some old memory, not some old guilt or fear.

To this day, I still use that tool to discard negative thoughts or beliefs that are hurtful or self-destructive. Even though I don't experience the ugly feelings, I still honor my past and know it is part of my fabric. I honor myself; I have made it past the pain and fear. I own my fabric and I am stronger because of it.

Bad things or good things are not who we are; it is just part of our fabric. It has given me wisdom that I use every day. I love who I am and am grateful for the compassionate woman I have become.

I am a very visual person and I need to have things to touch and look at. This is one of my favorite activities I created to honor my greatest joys and my deepest sorrows. I knew this would allow me to celebrate as well as honor the wisdom from my pain and release the negative energy. It is also something beautiful and uniquely me.

I want to gift this experience to you, so you can literally create your own fabric. It is something you will build on and recreate over the years. It is you, beautifully yours!

Here is your assignment:

Make a list of pivotal moments in your life—happy, sad, joyous, hurtful. I mean, the big stuff. The things that you still often remember.

Make a list of 6 Joys and 6 Pains:

Joy:
1.
2.
3.
4.

| 5. |
| 6. |

| Pain: |
| 1. |
| 2. |
| 3. |
| 4. |
| 5. |
| 6. |

Selecting your thread/yarn/material:

Now, select different pieces of ribbon, fabric or yarn, each representing what you have written above. Then, literally weave them together.

I had one woman in a group I was coaching, bring me to tears as some of her fabric ranged from beautiful lace to barbed wire. I will never forget that moment of acknowledging how moving and beautiful her woven fabric was. Some people used mod podge to decorate a canvas or box. Some tribal members have painted their fabric, because that was their most meaningful expression. I love this exercise because it is another way of finding common ground in your tribe. It also is a physical reminder of how remarkable you are for making it through.

I believe that the universe demands that you own your fabric. Once you become an adult, you are given full responsibility to own, shape, and weave your own fabric.

Now for some tough talk. You could spend a lifetime sitting in the "I didn't have a fair childhood" or "I came from a broken home" or "I've made mistakes in my life because of my past." My advice to you is STOP! Stop doing that! It's self-destructive and keeps you in the negative space of "I'm not responsible for my *now*!"

Honor your past as lessons, even if your childhood was extremely difficult. Own your fabric! In fact, don't just own it; celebrate it. Today is a new day and you can begin to embrace your beautiful fabric right now. Wrap yourself up in it and feel safe. Your experiences are exactly what have brought you to this place in your life right now. You have the ability to weave your fabric with purpose. My hope for you is that you can celebrate your fabric, cherish it, and honor it.

It is not an easy task to take those deep-seated feelings of pain, loss and betrayal and recognize those emotions as gained wisdom. It takes time to change your lens to see them as true-life lessons. It takes one-degree shifts but you will get there. Your tribe will help you and you will help your tribe, and your shared wisdoms will be paid forward to help others.

What I have learned:

1. Your fabric holds powerful energy for you. No one else can unravel your fabric without your permission. Be fierce about this. Allow no judgment of your fabric, especially from yourself. Be gentle and kind with yourself. Nurture your inner child and thank them for their courage and what they have gone through. Thank them for this wisdom their journey

88

will provide to get to your now and to help others survive their journey.

2. You decide what you want to give power to and what you don't. There may be moments in your past that you are not ready to shed light on yet and that is okay. Remember that you will spend the rest of your life weaving your fabric and precious fabric takes time to create and understand.

3. This exercise is just one way of owning your journey thus far in life. Make it whatever you want and take time with it. I have coached tribal members who are doing a series of pieces to slowly acknowledge and love their journey. This is your time to honor you!

4. Whatever your woven fabric looks like, honor it. Trust me, it will simply transform as you take this journey with your tribe. You will begin to see even more of the beauty in it and in you as time goes by.

5. Please take pictures of your fabric, whatever medium you choose. We would love to post it on our website. It will be anonymous, unless you prefer to have your first name, last initial listed.

I leave you with this thought: When your time is done in the physical world, the fabric you have woven will truly have touched countless lives, lives you may never know about.

Celebrate that!

Journal:

What have you learned from this chapter and the previous chapters?

- Why BeingTribal?
- Common Ground and Affirmations
- Meditation, Faith, and Gratitude
- Weaving Your Fabric

Make It Visual:

What do you want your life to look like? Write words, draw images or glue pictures below to create your vision board. Have fun with this and remember to keep it positive!

What are some affirmations to add to your list?

List any new affirmations that you want to add to your wall, journal or daily meditation.

Tribal questions for your next meeting:

1. What am I working on?
2. What has been my biggest success?
3. What has been my biggest challenge?
4. What is a measurable goal I will achieve in the next 30 days and how will I measure it and celebrate it? (Remember, baby steps.)
5. How can I help my other tribe members?

Chapter Nine

EXERCISING YOUR RIGHT TO JOURNAL

"Go confidently in the direction of your dreams. Live the life you have imagined."

— *Thoreau*

I have heard many perspectives on journaling. Some people say journaling is too time-consuming and others say it is a true blessing. I believe that documenting in a journal is how we are able to reflect back on our progress, our challenges, and our victories in finding our way forward.

Journaling is a practice that takes repeating to get used to, rather like exercising. You may not like exercising every day but when you build up your strength and feel your muscles get stronger, you will see the results of your hard work. So, build up your journaling muscle and I guarantee you will find it incredibly rewarding in many ways.

94

When I started journaling, I spent the first five minutes each night writing. First, if I needed to, I would rant about my day, throwing away frustrations. Then, I began to focus on what was really wonderful about my day and any wisdom I learned. I would transition into what I was grateful for and any goals I had and than I would finish with my affirmations. Over time, my journaling has evolved into my own rhythm and it is fun and revealing to go back and read some of my old entries.

Every once in a while, when I feel like I am repeating a pattern in life, I go back to my journals. . The goal of universal wisdom is to learn lessons in each life. And… when you don't learn a specific lesson, the repercussion or consequence gets bigger and bigger and bigger until you have to change your behavior. For years, I played the dutiful role of a doormat in my relationships. How great was it to say, "I give and I give" playing the victim, center stage in my own drama. I was exceptional at choosing narcissistic men who were handsome, flashy, unfaithful, bad with money, and manipulative. Why…? Because I was rewriting my same story over and over again, staying in the same comfy pattern with only one outcome – heartbreak. Of course, I would be heartbroken. I was choosing losers to share my life with because somewhere deep inside, I wanted to be…you guessed it… heartbroken! I was repeating the same pattern with just a few ingredients changed in the recipe of relationship disaster.

Until the last time this happened. I had finally begun to date again and this time I had created a list based on all of my past *oh so sad* journal entries. I made a check list of warning signs because I had to change what rang my

95

bell. Yes, this story is dripping with sarcasm because, the life coach, the fundraising executive, the woman who teaches other people how to live their best life, could not get her relationship shit together. I was embarrassed, I was ashamed, and the best thing ever – I was pissed and I had enough. I was going to change my life by paying attention to the cues of why I chose who I chose as a partner.

Well, this journey took me back to my old journals in college and it was like watching a slow train wreck. Starting with "today I met this great guy," to well, I bet you can guess the ending. The phone call from the other woman or the trail of emails or secret identities online. The shorter message of this all-too-revealing story is that journals provide you with insight that you can miss if you don't pay attention. I have a strict check list that I follow now. It has served me well and keeps me from repeating my old patterns.

This process works especially well around documenting what you are doing well. How you are fueling your body, how you are moving your body, spending your money, meditating, creating boundaries in relationships, and so on.

As you take this journey with your tribe, it will allow you individually and collectively to see your growth as you become a powerful force of love and wisdom. Even if it is for just a few minutes, try to document your day.

To help you on this journey, at the end of each chapter hereafter, I have created a place for journaling notes. There are four sections: 1. What have you learned in this chapter and how do you want it to inform your journey? (What do you want to change and what do you want to keep doing?) 2. What do you want your life to look like and feel like?

Draw or paste pictures; you can translate this to your vision board later. 3. Write down positive simple affirmations about the chapter. 4. Tribal questions to answer. We have created purposeful journaling in this book. This will help you transition to more daily practice. I have repeated each of the previous chapters at the end of each chapter. This is where you can document any new perspective you may have gained about a previous chapter. The idea is to capture any wisdoms that pop into your mind that you might want to share in your tribe.

I recommend you really dive in and give yourself permission to make your journal whatever you need it to be. This is not a one-size-fits-all practice. Everyone journals look differently. It is not just about writing your thoughts or progress. You may choose to draw, paint, paste pictures, whatever you want to create in your journal. Some people create verbal journals on their smartphones and transcribe them one day a week. Make it the best process for you.

What seems to work for the vast majority of people is to take ten to fifteen minutes each day to write down what is going on in your life. If you currently are not journaling, I would recommend starting slowly, maybe just a few minutes a day. Remember, like a muscle, you have to exercise or practice your journaling work. I promise, you will be grateful for your efforts.

In the "make it visual" part, I recommend you describe to yourself what you visualize as you are in the midst of your chapter work. It might be helpful to draw or paste pictures of images you have in mind. This will assist you in creating your vision board. It is also important to include what feelings you have around any visual cues or pictures, so you remember why it feels a certain way for you.

Whatever works for you works for you. Please do not compare your journal or your visual cues to anyone else's!

What I have learned:

When you journal your daily activities, you are empowering yourself to keep motivated and set yourself up for success. You will value your personal journey more when you connect with yourself and see your progress. It will also keep that inner negative self-talk at bay.

1. ***Work to write in a positive sense***. If you have to rant to get out the negative, then do that, but just remember to end on a positive note with affirmations. You will retrain your inner positive voice this way. Remember, you are honoring yourself!

2. ***Be honest***. The ability to be self-reflective will empower you to own and solve your personal challenges. When you re-read how you felt or what you said, there will be an aha moment. You can identify what was going on and you will gain great perspective and, more importantly, *respect* for your own journey.

3. ***This is not a competition***. Your journey through BeingTribal is a walking marathon, not running a sprint. If you truly want to transform your life and help yourself and your tribe members, then you must respect the journey. Your tribe will provide you with accountability and perspective. Your job is to remember that this isn't a competition.

Journal:

What have you learned from this chapter and the previous chapters?

- Why BeingTribal?
- Common Ground and Affirmations
- Meditation, Faith, and Gratitude
- Weaving Your Fabric
- Exercising Your Right to Journal

Make It Visual:

What do you want your life to look like? Write words, draw images or glue pictures below to create your vision board. Have fun with this and remember to keep it positive!

What are some affirmations to add to your list?

List any new affirmations that you want to add to your wall, journal or daily meditation.

Tribal questions for your next meeting:

1. What am I working on?
2. What has been my biggest success?
3. What has been my biggest challenge?
4. What is a measurable goal I will achieve in the next 30 days and how will I measure it and celebrate it? (Remember, baby steps.)
5. How can I help my other tribe members?

Chapter Ten

ENVISIONING YOU

"A vision is not just a picture of what could be. It is an appeal to our better selves, a call to become something more."

– Rosabeth Moss Kanter

About twelve years ago I started making vision boards each year. I like to create them in November or December in preparation for the next year. This is a great time to get family and friends together to create their vision boards, too.

My vision boards are a mixture of what I want to accomplish, as well as what I want my next kitchen to look like. I have manifested my salary at my job, my ability to find balance around meditation, finances, and even the ability to paint the cover of this book.

Remember my fourth belief that everything is possible? It is. I have seen tribal members I have coached, manifest

103

scholarships, unexpected paychecks, love, travel. This truly works.

When you meditate, journal, create affirmations and began to decide what you want your life to be and make it visual on a vision board, you are sending out into the universe what you really want in your life, and guess what? You will get it. What you believe you deserve is what you will get. So, use all of these tools we have been talking about to manifest or draw into your life what you want.

It is fun to go back to your board and see how you have manifested it in your life. Please remember that what we fixate on we manifest. Keep your boards positive and full of light.

Each year I create a new vision board and it makes me feel like I am releasing sacred instructions to the universe. I now include my four words that I meditate on—Peace, Compassion, Abundance, and Grace. I find images that I think represent those words and how they feel to me. I write them on my sticky notes and in my journal.

If you want to fill your vision boards with items you want to be surrounded by, go for it. There is no right or wrong way to create it. In fact, a friend of mine created a vision book that she continually adds to. The key is to make something that feels good to you.

A word of caution. Please do not create your vision board to please anyone else. Manifest in your life what you want. This is for you only.

My call to action for you is to collect images that reflect the visual cues you write down in each chapter. Seek out pictures, whether you draw them, cut them out of a magazine or find them online. Forget about your logical adult self and follow what feels good to you. Once you are done, place it in an area of your house or office that you see every day but don't concentrate on it. Let it just be.

Since you will all be doing this as a tribe, celebrate this activity, have fun with it and make it your own!

What I have learned:

1. Make a list of what you want in your life. Love, money, new career, new car, great health, great peace, etc. Make a list on a piece of paper and walk away from it for an hour or two.

2. Make a list of what you need in your life and add it to the list above.

3. Think about how each of the items on the combined list feels to you. Is there a certain emotion that comes to you when you think about these things and write them down next to those wants/needs? Document any visual cues or images that come to your mind.

4. Look through magazines or online for images that speak to you on your listed desires.

5. Spend more time day dreaming about your list and what your life would look like if you had everything on it. Add anything else to your list that comes to mind.

6. Add any words that spark joy to your list.

7. Gather your supplies: Blank paper (this could be a large piece of poster paper or and 8 ½ x 11" piece of paper). Make sure you have scissors, tape or glue, markers, stickers. Gather your supplies to your work space.

8. Gather your friends together. This is a very fun exercise to do with a group. You can easily do this alone but it is a great bonding experience to do with friends. Start pasting your pictures, writing your words, and even paint on your vision board. Have fun with it.

9. Once your vision board is created, take a picture of it and keep it on your phone. Put a copy of it in your journal.

10. Place your vision board in a sacred place in your home or office. I have a tribal member who tacked it to their ceiling over their bed so every morning they looked at it. Just let it go to work for you.

11. Finally, at the end of the year, reflect back on what you attracted to you.

Journal:

What have you learned from this chapter and the previous chapters?

- Why BeingTribal?
- Common Ground and Affirmations
- Meditation, Faith, and Gratitude
- Weaving Your Fabric
- Exercising Your Right to Journal
- Envisioning You.

Make It Visual:

What do you want your life to look like? Write words, draw images or glue pictures below to create your vision board. Have fun with this and remember to keep it positive!

What are some affirmations to add to your list?

List any new affirmations that you want to add to your wall, journal or daily meditation.

Tribal questions for your next meeting:

1. What am I working on?
2. What has been my biggest success?
3. What has been my biggest challenge?
4. What is a measurable goal I will achieve in the next 30 days and how will I measure it and celebrate it? (Remember, baby steps.)
5. How can I help my other tribe members?

Chapter Eleven

PUTTING OUR HEADS TOGETHER

"Everyday think as you wake up, 'Today I am fortunate to have woken up, I am alive. I have a precious human life. I am not going to waste it. I am going to use all my energies to develop myself. To expand my heart out to others. To achieve enlightenment for the benefit of all beings. I am going to have kind thoughts toward others. I am not going to get angry or think badly about others. I am going to benefit others as much as I can.'"

– The Dalai Lama

This book is about making sustainable changes in our lives. It has been proven time and time again that focusing on one aspect of change at a time creates patterns in our behavior or what we call habits. In this chapter, I want to talk about the science of how

111

our brains receive information and create new behaviors in our lives.

Do you know, it takes repeating a task or skill 50 times to code it as a habit, but it takes 500 times to recode or change a current habit? Practice makes perfect, so invest your energy in you.

In order to change our behaviors, we need to integrate our logical and emotional brains, which translates into combining the power of our left and right sides of our brains. We are going to engage our neurons in creating new pathways to recode our brains to behave differently.

Our brains are incredible problem-solving machines, containing 80 billion neurons, and it is believed that one percent, 800 million, are active at any given second. Every time a neuron fires, it produces a tiny electrical charge. To show how powerful these every-second electrical outputs are, we could fully charge our smartphones twice every second.

Imagine all of our connected energy interacting with each other, exchanging energy every second. If you were to put your hand under a microscope right now, you could see the energy that surrounds your body. All things on this planet have energy and we are no different than every other living being.

Knowing that we have this electric energy connecting with everything around us, it is understandable how we connect with the universe around us and draw to us what we desire. What we think we deserve is what we will get. We are constantly manifesting in our life around us with our powerful thoughts and that translates to the words we use and the images we focus on.

Any neuroscientist will acknowledge that in combination with the nervous system and its trillions of cells, our brains are disciplined, well-organized machines. If you learn how to tap into yours, the sky is the limit. It's important to understand that our brains create emotions, discoveries, and breakthroughs.

As the psychologist Donald Hebb put it: "Neurons that fire together, wire together." Fleeting thoughts and feelings, leave behind lasting marks on our brain, which form the tendencies and views that make us suffer, or lead us to happiness. This means that your experience is part of your code that you can rewrite. With a little skillfulness, you can change your brain to benefit your whole being and everyone else you affect.

Looking at our brain like a computer program, we are a living breathing computer code. If you understand computer code then you know that you can look at it, rewrite it, and upgrade it. Our human brain, our nervous system, our body, our DNA…is a living code of experiences that continuously recodes itself. Changing your life is about changing and upgrading your code.

In fact, even the cells in our bodies are completely replaced with new cells in seven-year cycles. Cells die off and new cells are constantly replacing them. Our bodies and brains are created to be changing and evolving, which creates the perfect opportunity to practice life in one-degree shifts. Decide what you want your life to look like and feel like and then create it!

Another way of looking at our behavior is to focus on the skills we have learned since infancy. Everything we learn is a skill. The idea that you are born with a certain IQ and it never changes is an out of date concept. Your *intelligence quotient* **measures** your intelligence including short-term memory, analytical thinking, mathematical ability, and spatial recognition. It does not attempt to **measure** the amount of information you have learned but rather your capacity to learn. However, if we combine our emotional intelligence with our IQ, we are truly wiser in many more ways than we originally thought. We are a combination of all the skills we have learned today and that whole intelligence, or what I prefer to call wisdom, is ever changing. This is how we transform our lives. As you change and grow your skills, you are developing a deeper intellectual and emotional wisdom.

Time for Some Self-Compassion

How much compassion do you have for yourself? Self-compassion is more powerful than self-confidence. We can get stuck in beating ourselves up for not meeting a standard that we would never expect someone else to meet. Perfection is not what we strive for. Growth and life experience to gain new wisdom is where we want to focus. Self-compassion is the highest level of emotional intelligence. It is one of our most important skills.

Emotional intelligence is when you can connect with others or connect with their emotions. When I coach tribes or professional teams, I am turning up my emotional barometer. I try to turn up my emotional barometer to sense the pressure in the room. What is the body language? How are people looking at each other?

It is important to learn how to recognize your emotions and the emotions in others. You can be very smart but if you don't know how to talk with another person and make a connection then you are missing a vital skill. I see this more and more in the college graduates I mentor. Their level of anxiety is high when they have to engage interpersonally with others and not rely on their smartphones to communicate.

Emotional Intelligence means you know how to listen and share with other people. It means you aren't afraid to say, "I don't know how to do this," or simply ask for help. Asking for help is a healthy skill!

There are three elements of emotional intelligence:

1. Recognizing your emotions, both in yourself and others, is a powerful skill. Sensing the emotional energy in a conversation will help to guide your tone and intent in that conversation.

2. The ability to know what emotion you are feeling: "Name it to tame it" is another powerful skill. If you can identify what emotion you are feeling in that moment, you can use your skills to make a healthy decision on how to mitigate your emotion.

3. Identify and separate your current emotions from your past emotions. When you recognize the emotions and you know what emotion you are feeling, you can decide if that emotion is from this current situation or residual emotion that you are carrying forward. Now you can make an emotionally intelligent decision on how to react to your feelings and thus the situation.

Your Emotions Serve a Purpose

Fear, courage, shame, joy, love...every emotion has a purpose or message for us. The lifespan of an emotion is an average of 120 seconds. You feel it and you move to another emotion. You can see this in toddlers who are perfect at reacting to their present emotion. I challenge you to be willing to feel each emotion and sit in it for a moment. It's powerful to feel it, identify it, and move through it. It is incredibly healthy to be present to how you feel.

Being present and identifying an emotion can be challenging to do because we have very busy brains. We have between 60,000 to 80,000 thoughts per day. Scientists have suggested that women have up to 20,000 more thoughts per day. Those extra thoughts are of worry and regret and how other people perceive them. Women also talk three times more often than men do, with the majority being *chit chat*. Whether this is to verbalize their worry or negative thoughts is not clear, but women cultivate more small talk and internally they have a preoccupation with the idea that they are not worthy or are being judged.

In fact, research has shown that both adult women and young girls are more likely than men and young boys to make connections between bad events in the past and possible negative events in the future. It is also true for both men and women, of the thousands of thoughts per day, nearly 80 percent are negative. We hear the word "No" over 150,000 times in our life from when we are children to adulthood. Our first default is to assume the answer to any question will be "No." Part of this journey

116

we are embarking on is to shift our thinking and open up the opportunity for the word "Yes" as the answer to our questions.

Getting back to being present in our emotions, feeling them and naming them so we can tame them...when you put a word to a feeling or an emotion, it allows the brain to understand the cause behind that emotion. When you name your emotion, it forces the Broca area of the brain to connect with the amygdala in the center of the brain. Now your brain is suddenly and actively engaging the emotional side of the brain (logic + emotion = activity) and the two hemispheres begin to engage each other. You can begin to understand your emotions and recognize them, gain wisdom from them, and let the negative energy leave that emotion so you can logically deal with it.

Please remember to honor your emotions and do not diminish or discount your physical reactions to them. The neurological pathway for physical pain is the same pathway for emotional pain, even social rejection. Every time you feel like you were rejected or have emotional pain, your body experiences a physical sensation. Feel the emotion and deal with it. Move forward with the wisdom and let the pain float away.

I want to give you a real-life example of my experience. I was at a grocery store checking out and the woman in front of me was a young mom with her toddler and her husband. They were purchasing nothing extravagant and when she went to run her debit card for the small purchase, it was declined. The cashier rolled her eyes and immediately the woman looked at her husband and he calmly said, "Let's put a few things back."

Before he could finish, the cashier interrupted him and said loudly, "Wait, now I will have to cancel this entire order and recheck it."

Can you imagine how this young couple felt? Embarrassed maybe? I certainly have walked in those shoes where I didn't have enough money to buy all the things at checkout. The young woman started to cry and the husband kept apologizing to everyone for the delay, and I was completely pissed off at the cashier for not having any compassion for this young couple and not helping them remove a few items.

I had cash on me and shared quietly with the young parents that I had been in their shoes many times and asked them to allow me to take care of their purchase. The young father thanked me and the young mother hugged me. I gave them the change from the fifty dollar bill for gas. They grabbed their one bag of groceries and quickly left the store. Then, it was my turn at checkout. I stood there in front of the cashier. Do you think my emotional intelligence was turned up? Was I thoughtfully navigating this important moment to understand where this casher was coming from and using my emotional barometer to measure the situation? In an instant, I had transferred every immediately available memory in my life when I felt unworthy or ashamed of not providing for my family and I was ready to transfer those feeling onto her like a cream pie to the face. I let it fly and told the cashier she should be ashamed of herself, and guess what? I did the most awful thing. I made her cry. It was cold water to my face and I was ashamed of myself for being an ass. I apologized and the young cashier shared that she had just had the worst day and she had only been there for a few days and kept making mistakes and didn't know how to delete items from the purchase. The whole situation spiraled and emotions were running high.

When we are in a situation and we feel the fear of inadequacy or the guilt of not being enough, we can turn up our emotional intelligence and say the truth. I don't know how to do this. Let's figure this out together. Understand what the emotion is: My weak spot used to be feeling ignorant or not knowing the answer, so I would just make it up as I went along, or as most people call it, lie about it.

Name it – What am I feeling? I'm embarrassed I don't know the answer. I feel ashamed that I am ignorant.

Tame it – Why am I ashamed for not knowing everything? Be vulnerable and be honest.

Reclaim it – I actually don't know the answer or how to do this, but I can find out or get help for you.

Name it – This young couple was embarrassed. I remember what it was like to be embarrassed and I am angry for them.

Tame it – My anger doesn't help the situation. Instead, I can help them and try to find compassion for the cashier who was feeling ashamed.

Reclaim it – How can I help? Not jumping into the emotional moment, but rather turn up my emotional barometer to be present and compassionate.

We have all been in emotional turmoil, out of balance, defeated and have lost. It is what makes us beautiful. This is one of my favorite quotes:

The most beautiful people we have known are those who have known defeat, known suffering, known struggle, known loss, and have found their way out of the depths. These people have an appreciation, a sensitivity, and an understanding of life that fills them with compassion, gentleness, and a deep loving concern. Beautiful people don't just happen.

— Elisabeth Kubler Ross

When I think of the word 'balance,' I imagine a yoga class or someone standing on a balance beam—maybe even with one foot in the air, arms in front or stretched out to each side. In life we don't just try to balance upright. We strive to find balance in every way. This isn't possible. Perfection is not the goal.

Some days you are going to feel completely comfortable and balanced and the next day you may feel overwhelmed. Part of practicing life in one-degree shifts is to learn how you can set boundaries in each area of your life so you know when you are in balance or not. Whenever you feel you need to be perfect, please stop and remind yourself that perfection is not the goal.

When I feel out of balance, I will try to identify what emotion I am feeling, why I am feeling it, and reclaim my balance by putting it into perspective. If that doesn't work in extreme cases, I will do a quick check-in with a tribe member. I know they will always be honest with me.

120

Overreaction Is a Domino Effect!

Name any one of your favorite sitcoms and you will find a myriad of storylines that involve an overreaction that doesn't end well. It usually begins with an incorrect assumption about a situation. The story plays out that instead of just asking what is really going on, the over-the-top mistake is made, which garners audience laughter and applause. In real life, (audience not included) an assumption turns into a snowballing situation followed by complete overreaction, and often misunderstanding and resentment soon follows. Plot line: in real life, it doesn't often end well.

Managing overreaction is a great skill to have. I have a successful tool I created called the *Gas Test*. It is my go-to when I coach tribes to keep daily life in perspective. It is a great diffuser, plus the name makes people laugh.

The Gas Test

When I become super stressed out or if I'm in a situation where those around me are stressed out, I use this scale: One= I have gas today. I am going to burp or fart in public today; ten= I or my loved one is in a life or death situation.

Where does this situation land on the Gas Test scale? After I rate the situation, I decide how I should react and how much emotional energy to put into it. Where does this problem fit?

Often, what feels like a nine, turns out to be a two or three. So, I engage my common sense, my emotional intelligence, and develop a thoughtful response.

Taking drama out of a situation makes it manageable. It is the gift of perspective wisdom that helps you solve the problem. It will conserve a lot of energy and prevent the over consumption of alcohol!

Yes, I have overreacted from time to time and I try not to do it as often as I did a decade ago. But if I do flip out, I try to give myself grace. We are all human beings and we are going to make assumptions, which will result in mistakes. My advice is to write about it. When you have a bad day and you overreact, you should write about it in your journal. Be thoughtfully present about why you felt off-balance or why you "flipped out." What emotions were you feeling and how can you tame those emotions to reclaim your energy? Remember, it's only one day. Tomorrow is a new day.

Another thing to write about is what was going on with you physically. Consider whether you were emotional before you reacted? Were you feeling tired, hungry, vulnerable, or defensive?

My Gas Test is just one of many techniques out there. Remember, this is not a one-size-fits-all remedy. Even the old "count to ten" practice works when you need to un-engage your ego and make a thoughtful decision. It's amazingly effective. Your tribe will help you develop a tool box to work from too. You have tools of your own. Share them and figure out what works for you.

I want to address the lingering effects of overreacting or the guilt that we allow to linger on our shoulders. It is another waste of energy to hang on to. I want you to act like a dog and shake it off! What do I mean by that? You know when you see a dog that is nervous, it shakes. Any animal, when it is in distress or scared, shakes. It is their biological way of physically ridding themselves of that fear or anxiety. It works for us as human beings as well. When you are nervous or excited, try moving your body. Shake, dance or even simply take a walk. Sometimes I close the door to my office and just shake my body. I close my eyes and imagine my stress falling away like powder.

A few years back, I had the pleasure of chaperoning my daughter's high school drama competition. There we were in the host school cafeteria surrounded by hundreds of drama students from around the state. Each school had many young performers who had worked for weeks to perfect their pieces. The competition categories ranged from monologues to musical acts to dramatic scenes. These brave kids wore their emotions out in the open and were ready to be incredibly vulnerable. As everyone was preparing to embark on their long-awaited auditions, something amazing started to happen. Each school group started jumping around and chanting a song or cheer. I asked the drama teacher what they were doing, and she smiled and said they were getting rid of their nervous energy so they could focus on their auditions with more clarity. It was joyful to watch and inspiring to see how they were emotionally connecting with each other and laughing and celebrating that they had made it this far.

There was this tangible energy of infectious enthusiasm. As the day progressed and each student performed their piece, tears had been shed and high fives and hugs had been given, and everyone was back in the same cafeteria. It was almost time for the announcements of which student performers would be going to state, and once again they were in their groups chanting and dancing. They had all made new friends and compliments were shared among all the students from other schools. I have to admit I was overwhelmed by the warmth and courage these kids possessed to be in this space and put their hearts and souls out there to perform their pieces. After the victories and heartbreaks through the announcements of each category, students reconnected once again to congratulate and console, still moving about.

When I am nervous about a presentation or need to rid myself of anxiety, I turn up the radio and sing and dance. I channel the courage of those high school drama kids and I shake it off! Guess what song I recommend to my tribes? Thank you, Miss Taylor Swift!

What I have learned:

1. It takes time and attention to change our behavior and our habits. It also takes being gentle with yourself when the process takes longer than you think it should. It took me a long time to learn to be financially responsible. It took me years of paying attention to my emotional reasons for why I did what I did. My point is, be patient with yourself on this journey of changing your behaviors.

2. I know what my triggers are around fear, love, and shame. When I sense I am going to be in a difficult situation, I work to be proactive in making sure I am present in each moment to avoid being reactive. I employ my Gas Test and adjust to the situation.

3. When I meet with someone I don't connect with, I ask myself why. Are they displaying a trait I see in myself that I don't like? I try to find common ground

with that person because I am giving them grace and myself grace at the same time.

4. When all else fails, I go for a walk, jump up and down or exert energy to shake off whatever I am feeling. I focus on what I am grateful for to change my energy and tune into what was just happening in that moment.

5. I avoid toxic people. If all else fails and I can't connect with someone, I don't spend time with them. I put myself and my own happiness first before all others. Not selfish – self-full.

Journal:

What have you learned from this chapter and the previous chapters?

- Why BeingTribal?
- Common Ground and Affirmations
- Meditation, Faith, and Gratitude
- Weaving Your Fabric
- Exercising Your Right to Journal
- Envisioning You
- Putting Our Heads Together

Make It Visual:

What do you want your life to look like? Write words, draw images or glue pictures below to create your vision board. Have fun with this and remember to keep it positive!

What are some affirmations to add to your list?

List any new affirmations that you want to add to your wall, journal or daily meditation.

Tribal questions for your next meeting:

1. What am I working on?
2. What has been my biggest success?
3. What has been my biggest challenge?
4. What is a measurable goal I will achieve in the next 30 days and how will I measure it and celebrate it? (Remember, baby steps.)
5. How can I help my other tribe members?

Chapter Twelve

MAKING FINANCIAL SENSE

"Too many people spend money they haven't earned, to buy things they don't want, to impress people they don't like"

— Will Rogers

Money, money, money, money...MONEY! I can hear the O'JAYS singing in my head. Finances, money in my pocket, my retirement. All of these issues have created huge worries in my past. I have seen it be the gateway of dishonesty, broken trust, and broken relationships.

The first goal in this chapter is to talk about our emotional ties to money and how we can rewire or recode our brain to see money differently and gain wisdom with our tribe in this transformational journey. This is a sensitive area to discuss as we all have deep seated issues around money. If we never had money growing up, we have one perspective. If money was around us all the time, we have another perspective. They key is to find out how you feel about money and how it affects how your control of it. Some people have great financial prowess and learned from a very early age how to manage their moolah and how that affects their credit rating, debt, retirement, and so on. I was not one of those people. I had to learn the hard way... by first failing and then succeeding.

In this chapter, I am going to take you through a few questions I had to figure out and answer. It helped me and I hope it is helpful to you, too.

My first step was to figure out what money messages I heard growing up.

Was guilt or power used in the manipulation of money in your family?

When is the first time you felt good about something you bought?

When did you feel like you could financially take care of yourself?

If you have never felt like you could financially take care of yourself, what do you think it would take to feel like you could?

To create a new understanding of what you want money to look like and feel like in your life, we are going to walk through an experiment.

Imagine you have all the money in the world...describe what your life would look like and feel like.

How much of that do you have now?

Your first responsibility is to yourself. The next step is to ask for help. Who in your tribe knows a financial advisor to give you tools to create a new pattern of thinking? Remember, this is a journey of changing behavior and you cannot do this in a bubble. Trust me when I say you are not alone in this. Everyone has a story about money. Be honest about what feels comfortable at first and move forward in a new direction.

I have a dear friend who lied to her husband for years about her credit card spending. They both made good money, but she confessed the excitement of her fear of getting caught by her husband with the new dress, shoes, a household item, was addicting.

The real issue was her emotional relationship to money and how it was defined for her early in her childhood. She grew up in a very controlling household where she and her mother were expected to look beautiful and thin, the house always in order, and to be seen and not heard when her father was around. Being an alcoholic, he would leave when things were out of order and seek comfort in the arms of women. This would create pain for her mother, which was transferred to my friend as a child. Messages from her mother were "you are not good enough, pretty enough, and now your dad is gone again and it's your fault.

So fast forward 40 years and my friend who struggled to find her own identity was married to a very controlling man, they had four children, and her husband constantly compared her to other women. Her husband didn't drink excessively or sleep with other women but still restated those same messages from her childhood and her escape was to have some control with buying new things to make her feel whole for just a few hours in the day.

Our money issues are ALWAYS linked to our emotional relationships in our childhood.

Some questions to ask yourself:

1. If I knew that I could feel financially secure, if I was intentional about my spending, would I make a change?

2. What is the minimal amount of money in my checking account to make me feel safe?

3. Without looking at my current credit card statement breakdown, tell me what I bought last month?

Check-in on Materialism...

Here is the question...do we really need all of this stuff? Do we really need the big houses and expensive cars? As Americans we are over consuming every day.

Of course, I want to look well put together and I want to have nice clothes, jewelry, and shoes. I want my home to look beautiful. The question I should really be asking myself is, what do I really want my life to look like and feel like? What do I really need to be happy? Finally, will my life look and feel the way I want it to, if I only buy new things?

Where does all that money go

Before we begin talking about creating a budget, I wanted to take a look at how the average American family spends their money. So where does all that money go?

Per the U.S. Bureau of Labor Statistics, most of our income is spent on housing, transportation, food and healthcare. Then we move to more discretionary spending that includes clothing, entertainment and other miscellaneous expenses. This where money used to slip through the cracks of my budget. I also bought a lot of gifts for people, even when they didn't buy me gifts. I had to evaluate how I valued money and its emotional link to my life. I was focused on how little money I had and how much debt I had acquired. How I was going to change my spending habits, but I never created a plan. And because there isn't a money fairy that appeared when I couldn't make my bills, I racked up more debt. First, I had to find gratitude for what I had. That came one morning in church when a visiting lecturer spoke about our connection to money and how wealthy we are as Americans.

How wealthy are we?

According to www.worldwealthcalculator.org, if you make *$33,500* a year, you are among the richest *5%* in the world. In fact, there are *6.2 billion* people less wealthy than you.

My intent is not to wealth-shame you. I want you to truly think about your future and how you want your life to look and feel in regard to your finances.

The first thing I did to make a one-degree shift was create a budget that lists all of your income and all of your expenses. If you are hiding either one from yourself or your partner – today is the day to come clean. Create a plan and seek out a financial advisor for help. Many professionals provide free consultations. You can easily find help at your local bank or credit union as well.

I am a big fan of paying off debt and releasing yourself from the weight of it. You cannot transform your financial life and create a healthy boundary relationship with money, if you don't have a plan. Once you have a clear and honest picture of your financial situation the next step is to begin to create a savings and even an investment plan. I have no doubt that women in your tribe will have resources and stories to share.

Even if you feel your finances are out of control, you are not alone and facing it is the like ripping off a bandage. It is going to hurt and then it will get better over time. Each step after your first will be much easier. It takes courage to decide to take control of your finances and you need to give yourself grace and compassion as you take this journey.

These are great questions to answer in your journal and share with your tribe.

What are some ways you can cut your spending? What has worked for you?

Do you have a budget? How do you stick to it?

Do you have a savings account? How did it start and how do you grow it?

Do you have an investment plan? How did you start it?

What questions or concerns keep you up at night around money?

What has helped me:

1. I had to decide what was more important, peace of mind or a new purse, or worse, lending someone money to make them happy when I didn't have it to give. I put myself first.

2. I created a budget of everything owed. I forced myself to track every dollar I spent and then updated my budget because I didn't even know where my money was going. Now I have the EveryDollar app on my phone because I know exactly where all of my money is and how much I have left each month to invest. It allows me to have peace of mind and feel safe.

3. I honor my hard work by making my money stretch and I enjoy being frugal. I rarely buy new and am thrilled by the deals I get. That doesn't mean I don't

splurge on a dinner out or a new pair of shoes, but I have a budget for that so it is not unexpected.

4. I don't make purchases over $250 without pre-planning or thinking about it for 24-hours. It's my financial check-in. We all have experienced buyer's remorse. My 24-hour rule helps me to avoid it.

5. I acknowledge that buying things for other people does not make them love me any more than they already do. Gifts are wonderful but not in a currency exchange for love.

6. I put myself and my needs first. I am self-full!

Journal:

What have you learned from this chapter and the previous chapters?

- Why BeingTribal?
- Common Ground and Affirmations
- Meditation, Faith, and Gratitude
- Weaving Your Fabric
- Exercising Your Right to Journal
- Envisioning You
- Putting Our Heads Together
- Making Financial Sense.

Make It Visual:

What do you want your life to look like? Write words, draw images or glue pictures below to create your vision board. Have fun with this and remember to keep it positive!

What are some affirmations to add to your list?

List any new affirmations that you want to add to your wall, journal or daily meditation.

Tribal questions for your next meeting:

1. What am I working on?
2. What has been my biggest success?
3. What has been my biggest challenge?
4. What is a measurable goal I will achieve in the next 30 days and how will I measure it and celebrate it? (Remember, baby steps.)
5. How can I help my other tribe members?

Chapter Thirteen

PAINTING YOUR OWN HOUSE

"When you say 'yes' to others, make sure you are not saying 'no' to yourself."

— *Paul Coehlo*

There are many theories as to why women take care of everyone else before they take care of themselves. In my many years of mentoring young women, I have talked about the concept of painting our own house. What I mean by that is putting our needs first, then family needs, and so on.

I speak from experience when I say it is very easy to pay attention to everyone else's needs rather than dealing with our own. Yes, women are natural nurturers and caregivers; it is part of our nature. We are consistently responding to other people's needs above meeting our own. This can keep us in a very reactive emotional place and the outcome is an empty-of-energy feeling. Following this practice, we don't take the time to care for our own feelings, health, finances... Need I go on?

I'm going to say something unpopular here. Taking care of everyone else is also a great way to be a martyr and build resentment for others because they don't recognize our incredibly selfless commitment to serve them. *I work, and I slave to make ends meet and no one recognizes or thanks me.* I hear my mother's voice and her mother's voice and so on. It's very well recited mom language. "Poor me" is something our egos love to live in. It is so much easier to build resentment than to create our own boundaries.

We don't have to do it all. Women are born overachievers, because for centuries we were taught that we were second-class and simply existing wasn't enough. We needed to prove our right to vote, speak, earn, and lead. There isn't a rule in the universe or from God saying that a woman is less than a man. We are in charge of how we live our lives; no one else determines our worth, unless we allow them to. This is a time to pivot our thinking on what we want our lives to look and feel like. The idea that we can be perfect is incredibly unhealthy, yet we set ourselves up for the idea of balancing it all and being perfect. When we don't meet our impossible standards, we blame ourselves, our partners (or lack thereof), and everyone else around us. We blame ourselves for not being perfect when perfection is not possible. We may have perfect moments, such as when an Olympic athlete who dedicates thousands of hours to one performance, and in that one moment, they are perfect.

Women are exceptional at judging ourselves against each other in unhealthy ways. I believe this is why there is a level of unhealthy competition amongst women. We undermine each other, because we are unhappy, so we need someone to blame. I have seen women cannibalize relationships with other women to find a better partner or job, more money, or more fame. The mean girl syndrome has culminated into an approved entertainment for our society to enjoy. We created it by unempowering ourselves to please society and allowing "likes" and "shares" to be our motivation. When did being thin and rich and famous become more important than being loving and wise and kind? When did undermining each other as women become easier and more entertaining than lifting each other up? We created this reality TV world we live in with all of our beautiful bodies hanging out of our clothing, literally disintegrating our value as human beings. Our human currency of self-worth is in crisis just as much as our economy of kindness, love, and compassion.

So how do we fix this? We put ourselves first and we change our beliefs about our own worthiness. This, too, is a practice of one-degree shifts. We, as women, must decide what we want our life to look and feel like and stand for. If nothing else, for our daughters and granddaughters. I believe we have to be courageous. I think we have to treat this like our life depended on it.

Mary, a dear friend of mine was in her last year of cancer treatment. She had been very open about her terminal diagnosis and we were talking one day about courage. I said that I was in awe of her joy and her courage to keep moving forward. She said, "Do you know what courage looks like?" I was caught off guard by her question and I gave her a basic answer about not being afraid, and she told me I was wrong.

She recalled sitting in the oncologist's office, getting her latest diagnosis and learning that her cancer was spreading faster than they thought. She said a social worker came in to meet with her and said, "With your prognosis... (repeating) with your *limited* prognosis."

My friend Mary stopped her and said, "Don't say that to me. My prognosis is what I make it. Every day, I get up and move forward. I get up and move forward, and I determine what my day is going to be like and what I'm going to do in that day."

Mary explained to me that it is the same as someone who is dealing with a challenging situation, whether a difficult divorce, overwhelming debt, or other situation where you feel frozen by the stress. You either make the decision to hide from reality or you make the decision to move forward, one step at a time. She looked at a quote I had on my wall:

> "If you can't fly, then run, if you can't run,
> then walk, if you can't walk, then crawl,
> but whatever you do, you have to keep
> moving forward."
>
> – Martin Luther King, Jr.

She continued, "It's our determination, our will to move forward that will get us to the next day. This is also true when we feel we are too lost to find our way home. Have faith in yourself. You do have the courage inside you to get up and move forward, to get up and move forward, to *get up and move forward."*

That truly is courage, recognizing you don't feel strong and you are going to move forward anyway. You make the decision that you are not going to let your circumstances/ego/self-doubt weigh you down and stop you from living.

Being courageous can also be your decision to pause in the moment and ask why you are moving forward. As you yourself if what you are doing feels right to you and if you are being self-full. Give yourself permission to love you first, then everyone else. Think about the wisdom you are gaining and write about it. It is so very important to push yourself to do bold things. For yourself, for your family, for your community. Make sure you are balanced first to prepare you to take action. Part of transforming our world after our self and our family is our community and I believe in giving back when my house is painted.

In the end, isn't love and wisdom exactly what we are truly meant to give to each other? Give love to our fellow human beings and pass on our wisdom to our family, our community, and our world? Please be mindful that your love and wisdom first nourishes your soul before you nurture or nourish anyone else.

In this chapter, I am going to share how I think we get off track and how we can get back on track by aligning our priorities and actions with how I believe we want to live. Discovering our own worth:

If we expect others to value our voices and our perspectives, then we need to do the same. We need to respect our minds, our bodies, and our integrity. I am a big fan of Gabrielle Bernstein, Jen Sincero, Brene

Brown, and Rachel Hollis, all amazing female authors and thought leaders. While I was searching online for amazing women to reference for an upcoming coaching session, I came across an article by Jenni Klock Morel entitled '14 things Badass Self-Respecting Women Never Do,' and I had to share... I have chosen a few of the 14 below; they are paraphrased, and I think they are great points for how we represent ourselves, and how we can change our self-perceptions and the perceptions of those around us. You can find the article on bolde.com. These are ones that I work to live by and they have taken me from victimhood to owning my own life and living the hell out of it.

1. We don't feel sorry for ourselves. We lean into the pain and move forward.
2. We don't over apologize. We offer sincere apologies but don't apologize for existing or feeling anything.
3. We don't please people at our own expense. We put ourselves first because that ensures that we live life by our own standards.
4. We don't body shame ourselves or systematically destroy our own self-worth with cruel and harmful self-talk.
5. We don't take piece of crap exes back. We learn from the relationships and we add to our lists of what we will never tolerate again. We make better choices.
6. We don't bitch or shame talk other women. We also stay away from women who do. We serve to share gratitude and lift each other up.

149

Understanding our motivation for seeking praise:

I used to spend a great deal of time helping others before I would spend time helping myself or focusing on my family's immediate needs. Why? Because I wanted praise and outside affirmations that I was good enough.

Our partners or children don't stand up and thank us for the income we bring in, the clean house we maintain, the laundry we continue to wash, the cooking, kisses, hugs, and so on. That does not mean it is not appreciated. My children have never applauded me for my daily contributions, given me a plaque, and recognized me in public for paying all the bills on time. Were they grateful for living in a home where the utilities were paid, and food was present? Of course they were. Do we need to remind them to share their gratitude with us? Yes, because we are the parents and we need to teach them to thank us for what they are already grateful for. If we practice gratitude in our lives, we also need to teach it to our children. I always sought opportunities to volunteer in my community because I wanted to make a difference, and deep down, I craved acknowledgement, love, and adoration.

I didn't grow up in a home where my parents appreciated each other and showed it. Gratitude is a learned skill of awareness of the good around us. It is also something we need to model. To share what we are grateful for with our children or partner is a great way to authentically begin a conversation around communicating gratitude in the home.

Please don't misunderstand what I am saying... I believe it is very important to make a difference through volunteering; however, we need to make sure our own needs and our family's needs are met first.

If we are putting all our extra energy into volunteering in our community, where is the extra energy to take care of ourselves? The answer is, without a thoughtful balance, there isn't any energy left for us. And whose fault is that? It is our fault.

When we are not taking care of ourselves, it can become challenging in the long-term because we end up resentful and burnt out. We can oftentimes put our mental, physical or emotional health in jeopardy.

How do you make a one-degree shift back to focusing on yourself first? I invite you to take an inventory of the time you spend each day focused on you. Make a list of how you could provide more self-care in your life. This is very serious because it will change every other aspect of your life. Can you find five minutes in the morning to meditate? How are you moving your body and what are you fueling your body with? Are you sleeping enough? We will discuss more in the next chapter. Once you create a list of what you could add to your day, then decide how much time you have for your family. Then decide what discretionary time you have left to give to your community. This is a great conversation to have with your partner and your family. I promise you that they are feeling your lack of self-gratitude and self-care.

Remember the oxygen mask message that we hear on the airplane before takeoff? In case of an emergency, place the oxygen mask on yourself before assisting others. The challenge is that we are not in an emergency situation every day, or are we? We are functioning so quickly with

24-hour news, smartphones, social media, and the like, it is causing heightened anxiety in our lives. I want you to make this a priority for you and your tribe. This is not being selfish; this is being self-full.

Here is a simple suggestion to take care of yourself. Keep a schedule. I know you are saying, "Um, excuse me but I do have a schedule and there is no time for me." I suggest that you start by prioritizing your needs first. Then add your family needs, your work needs, and do an inventory of what is left. Make sure the help you give others is not taking away from your time or your family time just to feed your ego. Remember, you are setting an example for your family (especially your children). When you set the example of placing a priority on yourself, it provides cues and guides for your partner and your children to do the same, which creates a healthier family unit.

Make a list of practical ways you can put yourself first.

How can you make each item listed above a daily or weekly habit?

Remember, it takes repeating a task or skill 50 times to code it as a habit, but it takes 500 times to recode a current habit. Practice makes perfect, so invest your energy in you.

Invest in You

Make a list of what you need to include or exclude in your life to create a healthier you. Commit to it and track it in your journal.

List what you want to focus on in your journal. If you and your tribe are focusing on one area, such as fitness or eating, write about what you ate or your workout and what it felt like. Journaling is a proven method of keeping track of what is happening in your life and the key is connecting how you are feeling about it. What is your emotional relationship to this change of habit or one-degree shift you are making? Yes, it will take time, and yes you have to pay attention to what is happening in your life. But it is an investment in yourself. No one else is going to invest this kind of time and energy in you. There is a huge payoff with journaling and tracking your life. It gives you feedback to share with your tribe and gain their wisdom around challenges you are having and sharing the wisdom you have gained and documented in your journaling process! So…make a list of what you want to focus on in your journal. Below is an actual example of one of my journaling entries:

Eating Healthy:
5/2010 - My intention today was to eat healthy and then it was Heather's birthday party and I started the "I deserve a little reward talk" in my head. Proud of myself for only having a small piece of cake and I even scraped off the icing, so I'm giving myself credit for that. Okay, so I did have another piece at 2pm, but I put it in my mouth and chewed it up and spat is out. Gross I know! My remedy was to drink another bottle of water – 33 oz, and I walked Tara for an extra 45 minutes. I'm going to call this a win.

Moving my booty:
Yes…I walked Tara. I tried jogging for a while. God…it would be great if I didn't fear peeing my pants with every move. One sneeze and I would have been f*&%ed.

I want a body that is tone (add to vision board – new pic "strong is the new skinny")
Do a monthly trade with Maureen – free ravioli dinner for 4 in exchange for massage
Commit to 30 minutes of some type of exercise a day
Meditate more consistently
Hydrate everyday – wine on Wed, Saturday and Sunday only
Be kind to yourself – add loving words to vision board

Investing in yourself takes courage. The alternative is sacrificing the wellbeing of your body, your relationships, even your money. If you are not a healthy you, you cannot be a healthy partner, parent, employee or volunteer.

What has helped me

1. I did one kind thing for myself everyday
2. I asked myself why I was volunteering at each charity and chose one that was the most important to me and resigned from all the others.
3. I explained to my family what I need to do for myself and they helped me find the time for me to be self-full.
4. I turned off the television, turned on music instead
5. I read more books that inspired me.
6. I loved myself and was grateful for my strength to put me first and my family in supporting me.

Journal:

What have you learned from this chapter and the previous chapters?

- Why BeingTribal?
- Common Ground and Affirmations
- Meditation, Faith, and Gratitude
- Weaving Your Fabric
- Exercising Your Right to Journal
- Envisioning You
- Putting our Heads together
- Making Financial Sense
- Painting Your Own House.

Make It Visual:

What do you want your life to look like? Write words, draw images or glue pictures below to create your vision board. Have fun with this and remember to keep it positive!

What are some affirmations to add to your list?

List any new affirmations that you want to add to your wall, journal or daily meditation.

Tribal questions for your next meeting:

1. What am I working on?
2. What has been my biggest success?
3. What has been my biggest challenge?
4. What is a measurable goal I will achieve in the next 30 days and how will I measure it and celebrate it? (Remember, baby steps.)
5. How can I help my other tribe members?

Chapter Fourteen

INSIDE OUT STRENGTH

You never know how strong you are until being strong is the only choice you have.

~Cayla Mills

We are beautiful, amazing creatures. Not only do we have amazing thinking and reasoning machines with our brain, we have also been given the pleasure of living in our human body. A body that was designed to be strong and resilient beyond belief and yet extremely delicate to the environment we live in. We can either nourish our bodies or poison them. We can rest our bodies or exhaust them.

Since this is the only body we have in this life, aren't we obligated to pause and pay attention to how we rest, move, fuel, care for, and love it? Our brain and body are designed to send us signals when potential problems arise, and we need to be attuned to their signals.

160

The importance of honoring our bodies is critical because if our bodies are healthy, this allows our minds to be healthy and allows us to be our best selves.

I have always struggled with my emotional attachment to my body and how I fuel and move it. The only way I was able to break my emotional connection to food by visualizing my body as a biological machine. It took the emotion out of it...most of the time.

There are many renowned experts on balanced diets and exercise plans available, so this chapter will be primarily focused on how we "manage" our biological machines to be the very best selves we can be.

You need to own your body and take charge of it like it is your most valuable possession. You need to nourish it and protect it from harm or injury. Another way to think about it: Ask yourself, what is your most valuable possession? Is it your car? Is it your home? Treat your body like you treat that.

Checking In

Your first responsibility is to know the status of your body. Here are a few questions I want you to answer:

1. Do you feel good? Do you feel like you have a generally healthy body?
2. Do you have enough energy?
3. Do you sleep well?
4. Do you have significant pain anywhere in your body?
5. Do you have a regular digestive system?
6. Finally, referencing all the questions above, please list what you would generally like to improve upon.

161

It is incredibly important that you know how you feel physically, as this relates immediately to your emotional and mental health. If you do have a serious concern, you need to see a healthcare provider. You should know how much you weigh, your average resting blood pressure, cholesterol levels, and so on. Once you have your basic physical health information, you have a starting point. You now have the unique opportunity to start afresh! You know the condition of your biological machine and you can begin to create your plan to improve upon its operation if needed.

No matter where you are in your health journey, today is a new day! This is a guilt-free zone. Let's start with sleep.

Resting Your Mind and Body with Sleep

Sleep is vital to your overall health. Resting your mind and body is critical to memory retention, your weight management, and your emotional wellness. Sleep allows us to produce human growth hormone or HGH. It is the only time that we can repair our cells. It is also called the time of memory consolidation; this is how we are able to remember our life experiences from day-to-day. It is recommended that we sleep an average of six to eight hours a night.

Numerous studies conducted around the world have shown that lack of sleep will actually reduce our immune systems' abilities to fight off disease. If you suffer with sleep apnea or other sleep disorders, please treat this like a major illness and seek professional help.

Fueling Your Body

If we remember that our body is a biological machine, we can relate it to a luxury item. See your body as a luxury car. If you were to invest in an expensive purchase like a luxury car, wouldn't you want to put the best fuel you could afford in it? Wouldn't you make sure you got the oil changed as needed and tires rotated when required? In fact, wouldn't you take your luxury car to the dealership for regular maintenance? Guess what? You are living in your own luxury biological machine!

I love great food. Breaking bread with my family and friends is something that I love to do, and I truly love to cook big meals, serve plenty of wine, and finish it off with scrumptious dessert. I would make homemade ravioli and bread every Sunday if I thought that was a great way to fuel my body. But it is not. I cook big meals to show my family how much I love them, and I love myself more for doing it because it is my happy place. I can still cook big meals, but instead of loads of fat, sugar, and carbs, I can create fresh dishes and save those family favorites for holiday meals. I want to celebrate life and I want a healthy body to celebrate in.

As I have grown older, I have had to change how I eat. I had to start paying attention to what fuel I was giving my body. In all honesty, it took me a long time to come to grips with my emotional attachment to food. I grew up eating for every occasion. I ate when I was happy, sad, depressed, or celebrating. There is the ongoing lie that our culture tells us and most of us buy into. We learn that when we are upset, we should eat an enormous amount of ice cream, a bag of chips, or other junk food. The lie is that it will make us feel better and keep our pain at bay. Even worse, some of us use alcohol or other substances to take away our present problems.

We have been taught to abuse our bodies in some attempt to delay the reality of our life. We form addictions to sugar and glucose but it alters the function of every part of our body, including the ability to think clearly and stave off cancer and diabetes.

Of course, the nutritional experts teach that moderation is the key, but it is hard when you have a habit of choosing certain "comfort" foods to rely on. If it takes 50 times to form a habit and 500 times to recode that habit in our brain, the commitment to changing how we fuel our bodies will transform our minds, how our bodies look, function, and feel.

We Cannot Process the Processed

Our bodies were not designed to break down all the chemicals in the pre-packaged, chemically-enhanced foods. Our bodies, working as biological machines, see this artificial food as mystery food and store it as fat. Make a choice to eat foods that you know are fresh. It takes about ten days to get sober or clean from the food addictions.

That is how powerful and detrimental processed foods and unnatural sugars are. You'll feel better because you are not making your body work so hard to process the processed!

If you end up binging on potato chips one night, give yourself grace. Tomorrow is a new day. Simply recommit to the love and care of your luxury biological machine.

Keeping Track

A proven method to staying on course with any change in eating and exercise is journaling. Keeping track of your daily food and exercise practice is a great way to pause and think about whether you want to eat that donut. I use an app on my phone that is easy and I can track when and how I fuel and move my body. It's a great way to hold myself accountable and head to the grocery store rather than the drive thru! I will be hosting several experts on diet and exercise on my website and list resources that I have used. I am not a dietitian or expert of any kind, but I certainly have struggled with my emotional relationship to food and my shame in not keeping active. I had to make a one-degree shift.

If you have a compulsive addiction to food, please seek professional advice on transitioning into a new way of living. You are not alone; your tribe will be there to support you.

Hydrating Your Body

Water is key to our survival. Not only does it hydrate our bodies, it makes everything work better. By flushing out toxins and fat, it will help prevent headaches and keep your organs in healthy working order. Water to your body is what oil is to your automobile. Your car's engine will seize up without oil, so will your body without water.

The rule for water consumption for the average person is 64 ounces a day or eight eight-ounce glasses a day throughout the day. I will even go further, as I believe you should drink your body weight divided by half. For example, if I weigh 160 pounds, then I should drink 80 ounces a day. Green tea, iced tea or other clear drinks work as well. By hydrating our bodies throughout the day, we naturally flush toxins out of our systems and our brains work more efficiently.

Wine and Spirits

Try to mitigate the amount of alcohol on a weekly basis. I love a glass of wine or a great vodka martini once a week, but not every night. Alcohol disrupts our digestive systems, our sleep patterns, and our caloric balances. It is very easy to gain weight drinking alcohol on a regular basis. Just like how you fuel your body with food, moderation is key when you add alcohol to the mix. This is also true with marijuana, cigarettes, and any other substance that alters your state of awareness. Everything you put in your body or inhale changes your body. If this is an area that you do not feel in control of, please seek professional help to make a one-degree shift in this area.

Keeping in Shape Is Really About Nutrition

The performance and look of our bodies begin with nutrition. Eighty percent of having a healthy body is what you eat, and twenty percent is how you exercise.

It is optimal to exercise 30-60 minutes a day. Find something you like to do that moves your body. Walk, dance, play tennis, do yoga, run, whatever you enjoy. If you enjoy it, you will stick with it. Make it easier on yourself by paying attention to how you are treating your body and watch the transformation happen.

Exercise and Your Brain

Regular exercise is very important for a healthy mind and body. In fact, your brain is automatically programmed to release mood enhancing hormones and chemicals, providing emotional and psychological benefits. For instance, below is a photo of a brain scan before and after a twenty-minute walk. You can see with walking approximately a mile, your brain chemistry begins to change. See the graphic below, courtesy of Dr. Chuck Hillman showing results from his research study form the University of Illinois.

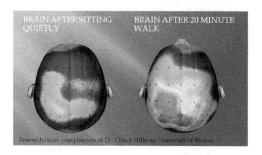

Research/scan compliments of Dr. Chuck Hillman University of Illinois

If we broaden our look at how the entire body benefits from exercise, a multitude of chemicals are released before and directly after exercise that enhance our emotions. Once again, if we are treating our body like the luxury biology machine it is, exercising is not about seeking a trim figure. Far more importantly, it is about increasing our happiness and ability to cope with life emotionally.

Striking a Pose

A few years ago, I went to a presentation by Dr. Patrycja Sławuta (http://www.patrycjaslawuta.com) who speaks about the Art and Science of Confidence; a topic I had never heard like this before. She speaks about your physical presence and the space your body takes up. This has nothing to do with your size, but rather your energetic presence and posture.

For over a decade, Dr. Slawuta has researched how our brains work and how our physical stances will initiate hormone levels to rise in our bodies. Your body communicates how you feel without ever using words. We are animals, and like any other species, our non-verbal communication shows more about our feelings than we can even verbalize. Our body language informs the mind and

168

actually informs the hormonal balance within the body. An example Dr. Slawuta gave was: imagine when you were a kid and you stood like a super hero and you showed off both your biceps. That is a simple power pose.

There's the animal power pose, too. If you look at a pack of wolves, how do you identify the alpha? He would seem bigger, right? What would he be doing with his body? He may have puffed up his shoulders, have a wider stance on his back legs. He is making eye contact with you. He is taking up space physically and it generates a reaction from all around him; maybe even an emotional response.

Let's visualize that you go into a bar and see a group of men; who is the alpha male? You can tell immediately as they stand in a different way from the rest of their friends. Women do the exact same thing. They stand in a different way than the rest of their pack.

Once again, a power pose is how you roll back your shoulders and stand straight. You make eye contact and exhibit confidence. All this nonverbal communication generates an emotional reaction from your own body and all those around you.

The same is true when we feel insignificant or insecure. We make our selves small. We shrink back, hunch our shoulders, and don't make eye contact.

There was fascinating research being done at Harvard University in 2015, using saliva samples looking at two hormones: cortisol and testosterone. Although the study was done on a male executive, it was also relevant to women and our bodies. Women have testosterone, but a lower amount than men. It has the same effect as it does with men. It has to do with risk-taking and confidence.

Nerves travel from our gut directly to our brain. This informs the brain if you are in distress or your body is functioning correctly. Harvard Medical School recently released a paper called The Gut-Brain Connection. "The brain has a direct effect on the stomach and intestines. For example, the very thought of eating can release the stomach's juices before food gets there. This connection goes both ways. A troubled intestine can send signals to the brain, just as a troubled brain can send signals to the gut. Therefore, a person's stomach or intestinal distress can be the cause or the product of anxiety, stress, or depression. That›s because the brain and the gastrointestinal (GI) system are intimately connected."

So how does stress affect us? It is with the hormone cortisol. If, for example, an animal is under stress, it will produce cortisol. We all have heard the research that cortisol in women creates an increase of belly fat, thus we gain weight. Cortisol, although an important hormone, in large amounts it is not good for us. Every time we make ourselves small, the body thinks we are in danger and therefore cortisol gets released. This is also related to how we speak. What happens when you are upset and try to speak? Your throat tightens up and you get a squeaky voice, which is created by cortisol.

The reverse is true, too. If the body is bigger, it generates testosterone. When we have confidence and feel good about ourselves, we stand up tall and walk with purpose. We make eye contact because we feel confident. Even if you are faking it, it will still create testosterone. Confidence is not being a showoff or boisterous; confidence is a grounded, quiet presence with charisma. It is feeling good about

170

yourself by the physical space you take up and the smile on your face.

In all honesty, fake it until you make it. If you are walking into a room of people you don't know, simply go up and start talking to someone. Even a short conversation and moving onto another conversation will create a confidence that will help with those pesky hormones.

I was sitting in my doctor's office complaining about my weight last year and how it has been creeping up. She asked me, "Are you working out regularly?"

I said, "No."

She asked, "Are you taking time for yourself to enjoy healthy food regularly?"

I said, "I am so busy with my work and projects that I—" I stopped talking and said to her, "I am such a hypocrite! I coach women to take care of themselves first and look at me?"

My doctor just laughed and said, "That is what happens in life. There is no magic pill or diet or workout. Just get back on track and watch what you eat and move your body."

It is simple: It is all about moving forward. Pay attention and be present to eating clean food and moving your body. I cannot tell you how many times I know I need to jog on the treadmill or do yoga and I don't want to. I would rather just relax. The decision we all have to make is to do something anyway. You will feel better if you honor your body. Even if your workout is less than great, just move forward and do it. You will be so glad you did. When you do, please thank yourself for investing time and energy in you!

What has helped me:

1. I keep track of what I eat and how I exercise every week. I am not perfect but I keep track because it keeps me accountable.
2. I pay attention to my stress level and take time out to nurture my body – even for 10 minutes a day. I give myself credit for trying.
3. I surround myself with women who are active, and when we get together it involves walking or some other activity.
4. I drink wine with my friends and eat great food and enjoy every bite. I know that tomorrow is a new day and I can enjoy wonderful food and friends without guilt.
5. I start over when I get off course.
6. I give myself grace and put myself first. Self-full.

Journal:

What have you learned from this chapter and the previous chapters?

- Why BeingTribal?
- Common Ground and Affirmations
- Meditation, Faith, and Gratitude
- Weaving Your Fabric
- Exercising Your Right to Journal
- Envisioning You
- Putting Our Heads Together
- Making Financial Sense
- Painting Your Own House
- Inside Out Strength.

Make It Visual:

What do you want your life to look like? Write words, draw images or glue pictures below to create your vision board. Have fun with this and remember to keep it positive!

What are some affirmations to add to your list?

List any new affirmations that you want to add to your wall, journal or daily meditation.

Tribal questions for your next meeting:

1. What am I working on?
2. What has been my biggest success?
3. What has been my biggest challenge?
4. What is a measurable goal I will achieve in the next 30 days and how will I measure it and celebrate it? (Remember, baby steps.)
5. How can I help my other tribe members?

Chapter Fifteen

RELATIONSHIP WISDOM

"Amazing relationships aren't about making one perfect choice in your choice of partner. They're about the infinite amount of choices you make in each conflict, each conversation, and each moment to open yourself and stay open, even when it's hard."

— *Vironika Tugaleva*

"Relationship Wisdom" is one of the longer chapters in this book because I believe it is critical to make sure you have the right people around you so and you can avoid harmful energy. There are people you have to have in your life and people you choose to have in your life. Your responsibility is how you manage your own energy, vulnerability, and perception around each of those relationships. No other person can make you feel a certain way; however, they can be a positive or negative influence in your life. You

177

need to know what your clear boundaries are in your relationships.

How you choose to live your life and the energy you want to have in your life is just as important as the food you eat. A simple way to explain this is with a question. Are there people in your life that you feel good around? That simply being in their presence, you feel upbeat and positive? On the contrary, are there people that when you are around them, you feel uncomfortable or they drain your energy? They are emotional vampires. Pay attention to your energy responses like these. We all have the ability to sense positive and negative energy and we need to tune into those feelings and trust them.

To make it a bit easier, I have added checklists in this chapter as I believe you need to take inventory objectively of your relationships to guide your decisions.

I have listed three general relationships in this chapter, however they will work for a multitude of relationship types.

1. The "lover" relationship
2. The "friend" relationship
3. The "family" relationship.

The Lover:

Okay, let's start with the "lover." Many of my friends have amazing relationships with their spouses or partners. There is a shared love and respect for each other. This is not to say that they don't have problems or disagreements, but they work them out and give each other grace because there is a long-standing trust built between them.

The "lover" relationship can be a challenging one for so many. Most of us have experienced it and seen our friends go through the experience of losing oneself in a relationship. This isn't solely in a "lover" relationship, but it is mostly in this type of relationship, so I'm bringing it up here.

Betty and Barney

Betty is in a new relationship with Barney (*Flintstones* reference). Everything in her world starts to revolve around Barney. His needs become her priority and she is also always thinking of ways to make him happy. She believes if she can really be the best partner ever, he will, of course, return her love and be her best partner.

While she is submerging herself in the life of Barney, she is not making her own life a priority. How can Betty find the balance between giving to her partner Barney, and keeping herself the priority? How can Betty have a check-in for herself?

Has this ever happened to you?

Write down what you think were red flags on your part that you didn't see. What actions could you have taken differently?

179

Here is a checklist of <u>Dos</u> to keep in balance:

- ☐ Spend time with friends—without your new partner.
- ☐ Continue to do a hobby/interest that you don't share. (Don't stop doing what you love.)
- ☐ Have your own voice—speak up for yourself.
- ☐ Make plans for the future regardless of your partner's plans.
- ☐ Become inspired to be the best version of yourself. Your partner cannot be your inspiration.
- ☐ Try new things that are in-line with your core values. If your partner has a hobby, try it but don't change who you are just because you want to please your partner.

Here is a checklist of <u>Don'ts</u> to keep in balance:

- ☐ Don't become too dependent. Your partner cannot make you happy or sad. Own your life.
- ☐ Don't talk about your relationship non-stop. Make your time with other friends and family.
- ☐ Don't talk to each other all the time. Keep healthy boundaries.
- ☐ Don't live every life's joy online as a "status update." Life is not a competition of happiness!
- ☐ Don't neglect your other important relationships.
- ☐ Don't depend on your partner to "complete" you. Jerry Maguire was a movie!

- ☐ Don't turn down a great opportunity for fear your partner will be intimidated.
- ☐ Don't move from one relationship to another. Take time to grieve, mend, grow and be you.

It is very important to understand that every relationship doesn't have to end in marriage or a horrible breakup. Partners come into our lives for many reasons. They can be lovers or companions, and sometimes they come into our lives to learn a lesson and move on. Whether a relationship is a great lesson or the love of your life that does last forever, just remember to keep you as a priority.

When we share our time with someone, we truly need to feel out or sense our relationship. Do you like who you are when you are with that person? If you can be authentic and love yourself even more when you share your life with someone, then you know that person is a positive influence.

If the opposite happens and you don't feel or sense you are your best self, then it is time to make a change or adjustment in that relationship.

Women and Color Crayons

Women are really great at taking a picture of a partner and instead of loving that person for who they are, we embellish the picture of them to fit our perception of what we truly want that person to be. Instead of changing or growing ourselves to be the person we want to be, we project onto our partner and view them with our colored glasses. We resent them for disappointing us and spoiling our picture when they don't turn out to be the person we colored them to be. Put away your crayons!

I am in charge of my life and I have to honor my boundaries. To have the life I want, I choose to love myself more than I love another, and even though that may sound selfish it is *self-full.* Remember, the oxygen mask is great perspective in relationships, too.

The Friend:

The "friend" relationship is a hard one because we were taught to be nice as children and be friends with everyone. We were taught to toss away our inner voice when we felt uncomfortable around other people rather than simply not become friends with them.

Great friends have great energy and will lift your spirits, make you laugh, and remind you that you are loved and respected.

I think there are three basic principles of a friend relationship: honesty, trust, and compassion!

Honesty is not just about telling the truth; it is about how you are able to live your life.

☐ Do you feel comfortable with yourself around them, so you don't need to change how you act?

☐ Do they know your weaknesses and love/respect you anyway?

☐ Are you the best version of yourself when you are around them?

☐ Do you know they won't lie to you and that they will tell you the truth with love and compassion?

☐ Do you know where you stand, and do you feel that you won't be afraid to share your true opinions?

☐ Do you know that you can argue, agree to disagree and move on?

Trust is knowing they have your back and them knowing you have theirs.

☐ Can you tell them your deepest secret and they will never share it or use it to hurt you?

☐ Do you know they will always speak highly of you with others?

☐ Do you feel nurtured in your friendship to be your best?

☐ Do they introduce you to others they think you would really connect with?

☐ Do you know they will never feel jealous if you make a great new friend?

☐ Do you feel like even though you haven't seen each other for a long time, you still connect immediately when you see or talk to them?

Compassion is knowing your friend cares about your best interests and will give you grace and support.

☐ Would they reschedule their day if you were in need?

☐ Would they give you grace if you make a mistake and would they share their wisdom to fix it?

☐ Are they thoughtful about important dates in your life and help you celebrate them?

☐ Do they also recognize that your time together is meaningful, and it doesn't have to be every day?

☐ Is your friendship worthy of work and thoughtfulness, yet it isn't ever difficult?

We all have friends that are more defined as acquaintances because we do not have a strong connection to them. Remember to keep your senses strong and when you are not feeling great energy around someone, please moderate your time with them. Reflect back on the quote from Jim Rhon I mentioned earlier in "Who Is in Your Tribe:""You are the average of the five people you spend the most time with." This is a powerful statement and one you need to pay attention to.

The Family:

The "family" relationship is the most challenging at times because you can't often walk away from this relationship, even if it is hard or unhealthy. There are situations where, for your true safety and sanity, you have to remove that person(s) from your life but most of these relationships are about boundaries. Let me say that again: boundaries, boundaries, boundaries! And guess what? You have to set them for yourself.

We all have boundary issues with our parents and siblings as well as extended family. No matter what role they play in your life, the good news is you can simply set your boundaries and that will mitigate the toll on your emotional energy.

There are so many resources on how to deal with family, so you should seek them out regarding your specific area of concern. You can truly google any situation and find a myriad of resources to review. Remember this: You are not alone. Every person I know, literally every person, has challenges with one or more members of their family. I think this is our earliest opportunity to learn to develop our boundaries. First, we learn from our older family members who teach us by example, and then we learn to develop our own boundaries and we pass that down to the younger members of our families, whether we realize it or not.

Your first step is recognizing your emotions around those family relationships that are not healthy and to logically walk through why you don't enjoy spending time with them, and then you create boundaries to protect your emotional energy.

What do we want in our family relationships?

For this section I am going to create a fictional scenario around "Aunt Jackie." Aunt Jackie is someone I love very much but I feel bad about my life when I am around her. Although I only see her at holiday dinners, she rarely has anything nice to say and often criticizes me, using sarcasm as her weapon.

We want, in the very least, to be loved and respected by everyone in our family, including our Aunt Jackies. The best way to do that is to remember that we can't change others, but we can certainly change how we react to them.

So, for Aunt Jackie to know what you want, you have to tell her. Sounds scary, doesn't it? It is much easier to close off emotionally or fight fire with fire and be sarcastic back with plenty of eye rolling and dismissive behavior. However, that only hurts both of you.

People act out or behave a certain way because that is how they were taught to behave. Clear and healthy communication is not a common denominator in most homes so if you want to change your relationship you often have to teach it and then model it.

First, you have to state what you want by asking for it. "Aunt Jackie, I am requesting that you speak to me in a loving and respectful manner." It may take some time to transform your relationship into this new dynamic of love and respect.

Be willing to hold Aunt Jackie accountable for her actions. If you have explained to Aunt Jackie that you will only spend time with her if she treats you in a loving and respectful manner, then you have to prove it. When she violates that by being condescending or rude, you have to tell her, "You are being really disrespectful, and I won't allow you to speak to me that way." Remember, many people actually don't know how to speak kindly or lovingly. So, model this behavior. Be kind and compassionate at first while still holding firm to your boundaries. This may take several times, but continue to walk your talk.

Next, if Aunt Jackie is still disrespectful, then tell her you really need to create some space between the two of you because she is not respecting your boundaries. Do this in a very loving and respectful way. You may actually be teaching Aunt Jackie something. You might reach out to Aunt Jackie and ask her why she speaks to you in that way. This may be the only way she knows how to communicate. If there is a way to open a dialogue with her while keeping your boundaries, then this could help guide Aunt Jackie to setting up her own boundaries. Finally, if Aunt Jackie isn't going to budge and is going to continue to be disrespectful, then you really have to separate yourself from spending time with her. Don't sit by her at family dinners. Still be kind, loving, and respectful but keep your boundaries.

If that doesn't work, you have to really think about your time and energy at family gatherings. If you need to mitigate your time and energy, then do so. Your emotional energy and emotional health is far more important than receiving a regular negative dose of "you are not good enough."

You can simply decide to love your family and compassionately know they will never change; however, you can change your response to them and realize the importance of how their opinion plays a role in your life.

Once again, there are so many resources out there and wonderful books on family dynamics. If you are in a very challenging family dynamic then please reach out for professional help.

Relationships are so important to our humanity and health. We need to be careful about how we create boundaries to be the best person we can be. Don't create your life around someone else's, because in the end, you will be unfulfilled and resent them for it.

What has helped me:

1. I pay attention to how I feel around people and avoid toxic personalities. If they are family, I mitigate my time with them carefully.

187

2. I stopped allowing guilt to guide my decision on how I relate to my parents. I ask myself what is best for me and then I follow the direction.
3. I put myself first. I am self-full and I work hard on it around my family.

Your most important relationship is with yourself. Give yourself grace and remember that all these wonderful lessons in life become wisdom we can pay forward.

Journal:

What have you learned from this chapter and the previous chapters?

- Why BeingTribal?
- Common Ground and Affirmations
- Meditation, Faith, and Gratitude
- Weaving Your Fabric
- Exercising Your Right to Journal
- Envisioning You
- Putting our Heads together
- Financial Sense
- Painting Your Own House
- Inside Out Strength
- Relationship Wisdom.

Make It Visual:

What do you want your life to look like? Write words, draw images or glue pictures below to create your vision board. Have fun with this and remember to keep it positive!

What are some affirmations to add to your list?

List any new affirmations that you want to add to your wall, journal or daily meditation.

Tribal questions for your next meeting:

1. What am I working on?
2. What has been my biggest success?
3. What has been my biggest challenge?
4. What is a measurable goal I will achieve in the next 30 days and how will I measure it and celebrate it? (Remember, baby steps.)
5. How can I help my other tribe members?

Chapter Sixteen

FINDING YOUR PATH OF GREATNESS!

Think like a queen. A queen is not afraid to fail.
Failure is another steppingstone to greatness.

~ Oprah Winfrey

When I first thought about writing this book, I thought I was going to call it *Finding Your Path of Greatness*. I truly believe that we all have a path to follow to bring love and wisdom to the world, which offers you abundance in life and also allows for a service to others to create a more compassionate world.

No matter what we do in life, our intention is to authentically better our life and the life of another. As beings, we generate an amazing energy that connects us to our world. We feel that connection in our soulful core and it is a powerful connection that intertwines our love to each and every being. When you are doing something

193

that creates positive energy for others, you feel a powerful connection deep in the center of your soul. That is how you know you are in tune with your greatness. I think this is one-way love functions in all of us.

Paying your love and wisdom forward and sharing it with others is our entire purpose for being here in this moment in time. It allows us to be transformational. Oftentimes, your path is a door that opens in front of you, and you need to walk through it. That is how my path in philanthropy chose me. I wanted to be part of something larger than myself, be a link to caring for others. My path allowed me to be a link between generous donors and critical care programs in healthcare, simply to help others pay their gifts forward, to be transformational. I've seen a food cart vendor do the exact same thing, as they brought joy into their customers' lives and created communities over lunchtime.

This book is my next path of greatness, moving past my fear with the help of my tribe to make this a reality. I know this works. I have changed my life and seen others change theirs, and I know that I couldn't have done it without my tribe.

194

I know that everything is possible. I wanted to purchase art for the cover of my book, but the artist wasn't interested so I painted my own cover. I turned on YouTube and watched videos on how to paint fire and energy and women in a circle and I painted my cover. Not because I am an artist, but because I manifested the ability to create an image that I knew would be fitting.

It doesn't matter what we do for a living, or what our talents are. What matters is our daily intention to be transformational. Paying forward your love and wisdom and receiving that energy back.

Are you paying your life forward by finding your path of greatness? Do you feel a calling in life? Do you feel like you can make a difference? We are all purposeful beings and your calling will be revealed to you if you allow it.

Receiving the Message

Can you remember a time when you were at a crossroads and out of the blue you heard the same message from unrelated people in the same day or week? Or, have you ever said something wise to a friend in need and thought after, "Where did that come from?"I believe we are all healers, teachers, and students. It is a sacred circle of knowledge, where we are always learning from each other. I believe that God or the universe speaks through us to share a message when someone really needs it.

Now more than ever, we have an obligation to vibrate or exist at a higher level through peace, compassion, abundance, and grace. We need to help ourselves and our tribes to make a difference. BeingTribal is a movement. One of the most important actions of BeingTribal is to take the wisdom that you have learned as an individual and a tribe and pay it forward. We created the world we live in and we need to change it, together.

Seek out your path of greatness and find a way through each of these chapters to connect to your higher self and your tribe. We are imperfect beautiful human beings with a great capacity to truly pay forward wisdom. Honor your own journey and take time to seek your higher self. Take time to process each area of your life and seek wisdom from your own experiences and the shared journey of those around you. Devote this time to yourself and your tribe.

In the end, you will find that your path of greatness has been right there with you your entire life. It's just been waiting in your soulful self. Make this part of your vision board. Give yourself a mission statement, be tribal, and make a difference for good!

Believe that LOVE is powerfully real and it conquers hate every day!

Believe that CHANGE can only start when you begin to love yourself more than anyone else!

Believe that we NEED each other!

Believe that EVERYTHING is possible!

As an adult woman, I am still transforming myself because I am continually discovering my strength as I journey ahead. I can honestly and unforgivingly tell you that I am grateful for every moment I have lived and the blessings in the wisdom that I have chosen to learn. Good or bad, every moment in this beautiful life has created the fabric of my being and I love my fabric. I truly believe that I chose to be born into this life. I have wisdom that I have fought hard for and I'm so grateful that I paused and bathed in it.

I am grateful for all the tribes throughout my life. Each one has added a thread to my life fabric. I learned so much more from losing than from winning. I have learned to be honest and authentic and that is a far more courageous path to take. I have learned that journaling, vision boards, meditation, affirmations, and self-love are wonderful tools to use in your life journey. I have learned to love who I am and who I am still becoming, giving myself and others grace in the process.

Today, I have an amazing and purposeful tribe. We are all lifted up by each other's love and courage, by our peace, compassion, abundance, and grace. We help each other while making one-degree shifts.

Changing and growing takes courage and repetition. BeingTribal with the right people and practicing life in one-degree shifts truly works. We are all one gigantic gorgeous human tribe. Like anything else, you have to start small… start with yourself and take one step at a time. I didn't know that in the beginning, but I found the magic along with my voice and beauty.

I have shared all of this with you because I want to help you honor your beautiful fabric. I want you to create a purposeful life and tribe. If you, too, want to discover the wisdom that you already hold and share it with others, join me in BeingTribal. Change your life in one-degree shifts with women you love and trust. Having those powerfully authentic relationships will change your life forever.

What I have learned:-

1. Love is powerfully real, and it conquers hate every day and twice on Sunday!
2. Change can only start when you begin to love yourself more than anyone else.
3. We need each other.
4. Everything is possible.

Journal:

What have you learned from this chapter and the previous chapters?

- Why BeingTribal?
- Common Ground and Affirmations
- Meditation, Faith, and Gratitude
- Weaving Your Fabric
- Exercising Your Right to Journal
- Envisioning You
- Putting our Heads Together
- Making Financial Sense
- Painting Your Own House
- Inside Out Strength
- Relationship Wisdom
- Finding Your Path of Greatness!

Make It Visual:

What do you want your life to look like? Write words, draw images or glue pictures below to create your vision board. Have fun with this and remember to keep it positive!

What are some affirmations to add to your list?

List any new affirmations that you want to add to your wall, journal or daily meditation.

Tribal questions for your next meeting:

1. What am I working on?
2. What has been my biggest success?
3. What has been my biggest challenge?
4. What is a measurable goal I will achieve in the next 30 days and how will I measure it and celebrate it? (Remember, baby steps.)
5. How can I help my other tribe members?

MEDITATION NOTES

These are my very personal meditation notes from a group meditation led by the amazing Joan Jerman in White Salmon, Washington in 2014. The question asked when the meditation began was: "What did you bring to share with your spirit guides and angels and what are you seeking?" We were told to document our visions and messages immediately during this meditation.

In that meditation, I brought my love and peace to share. I was seeking clarity to honor myself, and to teach others to respect and love themselves and each other. I was seeking how I could encourage women to be loving and supportive for each other. During the meditation, I had the following very clear vision:

I am with a woman, but I am the woman and she is me and yet she is also separate from me. She is who I used to be, and she is now in me. She is my soulful spirit voice.

She has been awakened in me to share wisdom. She is a past version of me. I see through her eyes but also can watch her. She is speaking to me, and she is part of me

203

and her voice is my voice. I am now alone but I feel her wisdom and love in me.

There is a man next to me now. He is ancient and vibrant. He has longer gray hair past his shoulders and it is pulled back away from his face. He is the father, the mentor, wisdom embodied. He is powerful and calming. All things start and end with him. He wears a light earth-colored robe and it seems to change color as he moves. It is beautiful, he is beautiful, and I feel loved and safe. He is holy. I have seen him before, but I have never heard him speak. He has no voice, yet I hear him speaking to me.

I am wearing a white robe or gown. It is floor-length or maybe longer and I feel like it protects me. I have a cloak or shawl over it and it is bluish or purple in color. It is over my shoulders and flows down to the ground. It is heavy and yet has no weight.

He takes my hand and we are flying, soaring, but I have no fear. He is next to me, guiding me on the wind, yet I feel no breeze. I somehow know that it is the common way we move. We land on the beach and I feel the sand under my feet, scrunching my toes. We walk over the sand to the smooth river rocks and I walk into the water. It is cool. I am immersed to my waist in the water, yet I am not wet. We walk through the water to a path and now we are on a mountaintop. I begin to speak but it is not my voice. It is my soulful spirit. She is speaking; she is so wise. I can see myself and I am speaking to myself. I speak, and I feel these words, "I am the sovereign. I have died before for speaking the truth and I will freely die again." I am aware of the light around me and it protects me. He protects me. I raise my hand to gesture to the man on my left side—he is always on my left side. "I am healing. I am the sovereign. I know what I know. I was immersed in the knowledge of water and I was restored by its wisdom. I am ready."

I have a knowing so steady it is calming. I know the universe is waiting for this truth. I must move forward and release it. I have been here before.

I raise my hand to my guide on my left and continue to speak, still in my soulful spirit voice. I don't hear her voice, rather, I just feel her words. I feel her words like a gift of knowledge that become my words. I say, "He is always with me. I have great power in love. I have great energy and I am meant to change the world through love and wisdom. I was chosen centuries ago and my journey continues. This is a continuation of my path, a continuation of the universe speaking through me. A continuation of light.

"Peace, Compassion, Abundance, and Grace are my prayers. I am the sovereign of Truth and Light. He is my teacher. He is my guide. From the water I emerge cleansed. From the water I emerge whole. From the water I emerge full of wisdom. I am lifted by the power of this love. From the water I am cured. From the water I am full of hope. From the water I am connected. My heart and mind are connected. From the water I am ready to teach. I am at the top of the mountain and angels of light lift me up and I am surrounded by spirit beings.

"I am flying. I am soaring. I am here to share. It is not my message. It is not from only me. It is from Love, from God. It is from a holy place. It is from wisdom leaders. It is from the water by which I was created. I am the water that I was created from. I am the energy that created me. I am the mountain on which I stand. I am the sky that I look up to.

"Do you feel me? I am within you. I am without you. I am the air you breathe. I am the ground you stand on. I am the sand on the beach and the soil the plants grow from. I am the sunlight that warms your skin. This is where the wisdom comes from. This is where the water is held. Listen to my whispers.

"I am with you, around you. I am the path that you are walking on that I have created for you. I am carrying you when you fall. Release it and allow it to be—to be read. Let it be birthed to the truth, to become living wisdom. This has been in you. You are the vessel that has been chosen. On the path to the water, from the water to the mountain, on the mountain to the sky, to be freed to all. It is now!"

SAYING GOODBYE

I began this book with sharing a recurring dream that I had for many of my teenage years. It was my mind's way, I think, of forcing me to take charge of my healing. To acknowledge my pain and seek help.

I end this book with how I forgave my mother, and forgive myself for such a hard life my soul had chosen and to become my own mother.

My mother was a woman trying to outrace what she believed were her misgivings as a woman, mother, daughter, and sister. Like every other soul on Earth, she was her harshest critic. She did the very best she could. Mom was becoming and growing into her soul. Like me, she had chosen this life to be born into. To struggle and learn and move forward with greater wisdom. My higher conscious self speaks these words to you. As I child, I just wanted my parents to love and protect me.

I lived almost all my life in gratitude of my Mom. She, too, was busy wallpapering the outside of her glass cover. I always saw her as beautiful and determined and loving. I don't ever remember watching Mom taking time to just love herself for the amazing woman she was, truly honor her beautiful fabric of loss and love, shame and courage. All of it. And I love her for working so hard to exist in her own skin and try each day to do the right thing.

It was Mother's Day in 2016 and I picked Mom up to meet my sister for brunch. The sun streamed through my car windows as I drove from Washougal, Washington to Gladstone, Oregon. The traffic was light and I was listening to Frank Sinatra sing Come Fly with Me and then Luck be a Lady and I looked forward to seeing my mom and my sister. I was not prepared for what was about to happen. I arrived at mom's house, wished her happy Mother's Day, said hello to my step-dad and off Mom and I went for the day, with the radio playing Tony Bennett's Just in Time. We headed off to the restaurant again and I asked one simple, unimportant question. A question that I didn't' care what the answer was, I just wanted to chat as we made our way to the restaurant down the road. "So Mom, how has your weekend been so far?" In that moment, she began to share how she had spent time with a man who had ripped my childhood away from me. The young man who had told his friend that he should try me out. That I was good. The man she hadn't seen in years. She started sharing how wonderful it was to connect with him. I could feel thick constricting air fall on me. Suffocating sand slowly doing its work to bury me in a silo without escape. My ears began buzzing, ringing. Suddenly her words were far off and distant. I was working to focus on keeping the car on the road and I shouted, "Please stop talking about this, please I don't want to hear about this, I don't care how he is!" But she kept talking as if she knew it was tearing me apart. I looked at her; how could she have a smile on her face?

The numbness set in. Fold it away, Rena, I told myself. You can handle this. My skin began to tingle, and the thickness of shame and guilt covered me. I kept repeating to myself, "You can get through this, you can get through this, you are strong enough."

Mom had reached deep inside of me and pulled out something I had killed long ago... a weed that sat dead inside. I felt like she had pulled it out of me, nurtured it back to a living thing, and shoved it in my face.

We arrived at the restaurant, my heart thrown into that fucking sock drawer but they weren't folded; they were crumpled and each sock unraveled like venomous snakes shedding their skin. This was poison to me. I was being poisoned and I was desperate for rescue. We sat down with my sister and I knew if Mom told my sister what she told me, my sister would rescue me and pounce on my mother. I would be protected, saved from the choking sand slowly burying me, the weight of the shame and guilt weighing me down. I would not survive this without rescue. I looked at my mother and said, "Tell Laurie what you told me about your weekend." Here it comes, the rescue... it was all some awful mistake. My own mother will somehow realize what she has done and apologize to me. Please someone save me!

My mother looked at my sister and said, "Oh it has just been a busy weekend." How could she do this to me? How could her cruelty tell me that I don't matter, that my pain didn't matter? I was nearly covered by the sand with no hope for me. The thing that should have been dead was alive again. Laurie called my name, but I didn't hear her. She called my name again and I came back from the grayness of that far-off place. "Rena, honey, what is wrong?" I didn't realize that my whole body had begun shaking and, in that moment, I lost my shit. In a public restaurant I began sobbing and screaming at my mother – "Why didn't you protect me? What kind of mother are you to sit there and tell me about your lovely time with HIM? I was just a little girl; I was a little girl!" I remember running out of the restaurant and falling in the parking lot, and I began to vomit. Next thing I knew I was in my car and parking in another parking lot, and then I heard the howling. The uncontrollable howling. It was me making that noise but not just from my mouth… it was from my soul, somewhere past where my lungs exist.

My phone began to ring. It was my sister. I was trying to answer, trying to talk, but it was not me; it was a disconnected voice asking for help.

It took several weeks before I was finally able to sit with my mother and ask why. In one moment, she seemed apologetic, and in the other she seemed as if she didn't know about my childhood and stories were switching between my sisters and me about what had happened. I had to move forward and the only way I could do so was to face the betrayal and find some sense of forgiveness. Then, a few weeks later, my stepfather said, "Something is wrong with your mother, she isn't thinking right," and I knew it was my fault for screaming at her. But it wasn't. Mom had begun to have more episodes of memory and other symptoms were arising with her balance. Mom met with doctors who referred her to more doctors. We were all trying to find some answers.

I was existing in two worlds. One, I refused to feel guilty for standing up for myself and knowing that I would not tolerate betrayal from anyone, and the other was a knowing that there must be some explanation of why Mom would be so terribly ugly and hateful. She couldn't just become a cruel person so suddenly. I needed answers. I needed something to hold onto to believe that all I knew was not a lie.

In the September, Mom saw a neurologist and by December 2016 and they suspected she had a brain tumor. Because of my work in healthcare, my stepfather asked if I would assist in navigating treatment options. And I threw myself head first into being part of her care plan. This is where I believed I could find that relationship with my mother again. It wasn't her fault at all, it was a brain tumor. That is what I wanted to believe. Mom loved me and always tried to protect me. That was always what I hung onto.

It was a Wednesday, January 11, during a snow storm, when we made our way to the hospital for the biopsy. That is the day they said the words, "inoperable cancerous brain tumor." Mom was soon diagnosed with Anaplastic Astrocytoma. It sounded like a woman's name, as if her nickname would be Ana. Could we reason with this "Ana?" Would she let go of her grip on Mom? Was this "Ana" a mother too, and would she surrender Mom back to us? The cold answer, just like that stormy morning was NO.

My focused shifted away from my own healing into the care of Mom. Mom found new focus and vowed to beat the cancer, and I along with her loving husband and my two amazing sisters plus the rest of the family were along for the fight. All hands on deck. This tribe was not going to allow cancer to take Mom away. That was our focus. I was good at this shit. I was tucking my tattered socks, and shoved them back into my drawer. I was fighting to forgive my mom, but I didn't realize that I was fighting to forgive me, too. Mom was going to slip away from us, and I began to mother Mom. I didn't realize until later that I was becoming my own mother, too.

Her mind was slowly being invaded and overtaken by "Ana," and in her lucid moments she worked to make sure that everyone knew how much she loved them. And how grateful she was to be their wife, mother, grandmother, sister, and friend. We went through days, weeks and months of radiation and chemotherapy in the hope that there would be a second chance, but her treatment poisoned her while poisoning the cancer, and she was left exhausted, weak, and frail. In April, Mom transitioned to hospice care. Mom was either childlike, adoring or angry. If the grandchildren were present, she was "doing just fine" and didn't want to worry them. The moments of cruel words and angry outbursts became more common. "Ana" was growing faster now.

In May, we met with the Hospice Doctor and it was a beautiful moment that touched each of our lives with wisdom and candor. For both what he said and how he said it. When Mom was asked by her doctors and nurses about how she was feeling, she would most often say, "Oh, I'm feeling fine," even if she couldn't even raise her head off the pillow. The hospice doctor had come to the house and asked Mom that question, how are you feeling? And Mom answered the same as usual, "I'm fine." You know in those moments when you see wisdom and love wrapped up in a being who is focused on easing the way of others? It was that kind of moment with that kind of human being with her hospice doctor. He asked, "How about I tell you the most common questions most patients ask me, and if you want, I will give you the answers?" Mom said yes and we were all nodding. We were hoping for the easing of words to navigate what was to happen next. He continued. "Most patients ask me how much longer will I live? Would you like to know that answer?" It was like all the stress left the room, and the air in the room lightened. I thought to myself, he just went there. He asked the question we all didn't want to ask in the fear that someone or anyone would think that we were tired of being in this place of watching *our person, our Mom* die. Mom relaxed and said, "Yes, I would like to know."

The answers and questions began to flow, and it took the fear out of us asking the hard questions. It was the perfect example of *allowing*. Allowing for truth to come in like morning light through a bedroom window. It warmed our skin and eased us to awaken to the truth of letting go. That afternoon we asked Mom questions about how she wanted us to celebrate her life, the songs she wanted us to sing, and scripture and poems she wanted read. We spoke about who she wanted to see in her final weeks ahead and anything she wanted to do.

There was a joy in this new moment of acceptance. It eased Mom's way to live out her time on this earth, in this body, the best way she could. Mom talked about how much she is looking forward to seeing her family in Heaven and then she fell deep asleep.

In the weeks ahead, Mom had good days and bad days, and it was exhausting and precious, heart wrenching and joyous. During Mom's last two weeks, we watched her slowly slip away. We kept her comfortable with morphine and she had many visitors. When you watch someone slowly die and you know their wishes are to let life take its course, you secretly grapple with the idea of overdosing on morphine to ease their way, but that was not what Mom wanted. But the guilt sits on your skin and you are afraid to tell anyone how you feel. But because of what the hospice doctor taught us, we had the courage and the *allowing* to share with each other how we felt.

My mother labored me into this world, and I had the sacred and precious moment to slowly and painfully labor her out. She died on Friday August 18, 2017 at 10:10p.m. She was lifted from her human form by her angels and loved ones and each of us girls now dream about her and feel her with us. She is one of our angels now. I loved that she left us at 10:10 because it is the Angel sign. It is a sign of rebirth and renewal. Of new beginnings and new lifetimes.

I didn't really howl again until we spread her ashes on a cold rainy day at the coast. We released her into the sea, and we walked to the top of the hill and I howled. I howled for myself, too. My mother was gone. The woman who loved me and nurtured me and the woman who ripped the dead thing out of me on that Mother's Day morning and held it up, to my horror. It took me two more years and the counsel of a dear friend to realize that as painful as it was, Mom ripped it out of me. That old shame I had buried deep inside is gone. Just as painful and cruel and heartbreaking she pruned my old dead plant with her sharp shears, now new beautiful possibilities were growing inside of me. I have learned to become my own mother. To nurture that little girl who was betrayed and hurt. I care for her now. I remind her of her power and beauty. I protect her and show her the magic of love and forgiveness.

I share this with you because in times of great despair and loss we can embrace our own pain and be our own mothers and fathers. We can speak the things we fear out loud and find the grace and wisdom in it. We are given the gift of witnessing life and death in many ways and it lightens our existence; through the painful and precious, laboring of a renewed beginning.

Each new day is in an opportunity to begin again. Laugh, weep, love, forgive, be. Cherish and labor through all of it. I wish you all of it as it exists in love.

ABOUT THE AUTHOR

 Rena Whittaker has been coaching woman and men to create and cultivate meaningful tribes for many years. She also serves as an executive coach, guiding leaders and teams to traverse through the work of discarding guilt, shame, and resentment and moving forward with positive visioning, team agreements, and authentic interpersonal communication, to achieve their best vision.

Additionally, Rena Whittaker has enjoyed over twenty years as a philanthropy executive and community changemaker. Her expertise in "restarting" foundations and community coalition development has empowered leaders and teams to think unconventionally and collectively.

Rena's commitment to coaching and mentoring throughout her career has helped transform herself and others through her passionate belief that "anything is truly possible."

Rena is the president and founder of Polallie, LLC and www.beingtribal.com.

217